Victory or Death!

STORIES OF THE AMERICAN REVOLUTION

by Doreen Rappaport and Joan Verniero

illustrated by Greg Call

HARPERCOLLINS*PUBLISHERS*

With love and "all that jazz," for Dani Rosegarten,
who has already started her own revolution
—D.R.

For my grandmother Theresia Brenner,
from whom I learned to listen
—J.V.

Victory or Death!
Text copyright © 2003 by Doreen Rappaport and Joan Verniero
Illustrations copyright © 2003 by Greg Call
For information address HarperCollins Children's Books, a division of
HarperCollins Publishers, 1350 Avenue of the Americas, New York, NY 10019.
www.harperchildrens.com

Library of Congress Cataloging-in-Publication Data
Rappaport, Doreen.
   Victory or death! ; stories of the American Revolution / by Doreen Rappaport
and Joan Verniero ; illustrated by Greg Call.—1st ed.
      p.   cm.
   Contents: The soldier with the pen : Peter Brown — The oath : Francis Salvador
— "Yours, Portia" : Abigail Adams — The decision : George Washington —
Tarnation Sybil! : Sybil Ludington — A question of justice : Grace Growden
Galloway — The spy : James Armistead — The recruit : Robert Shurtliff.
   ISBN 0-06-029515-5 — ISBN 0-06-029516-3 (lib. bdg.)
   1. United States—History—Revolution, 1775–1783—Biography—Juvenile
literature.   2. United States—History—Revolution, 1775–1783—Anecdotes—
Juvenile literature.   [1. United States—History—Revolution, 1775–1783.]
I. Verniero, Joan.   II. Call, Greg, ill.   III. Title.
E206.R37   2003   2002012837
973.3'092'2—dc21   CIP
[B]   AC

Typography by Hilary Zarycky
1   2   3   4   5   6   7   8   9   10
❖
First Edition

CONTENTS

ABOUT THIS BOOK

Late in the afternoon on Christmas Day 1776, the ragged Continental army lined up at McKonkey's Ferry to cross the Delaware River, hoping to launch a surprise attack on Hessian soldiers camped at Trenton, New Jersey. George Washington sent his officers down the soldiers' lines to rally them. As vicious snow and sleet swirled about, Washington wondered how his men could bear it, since most wore only the thinnest of coats and shirts and pants. The lucky ones had rags wrapped around their feet for shoes.

"Victory or death!" The officers whispered the battle cry down the ranks. The courage and determination of these American soldiers have made the crossing of the Delaware and the Battle of Trenton one of the "big events" that the world identifies with the struggle for independence in the United States.

Heroic acts were a way of life when colonial America went to war against Great Britain. But "big events" and "big people" present only a fraction of the story of the American Revolution. A more complete view must include not-yet-celebrated Americans, people whose important contributions have been forgotten. It must include the struggle among the colonists over the issue of independence, for many colonists did not want to separate from Great Britain. Whether one was a patriot supporting revolution or a loyalist siding with England, every American's life was affected. Here are stories of some of these people—some famous and some lesser known. We've tried to reflect the many cultures in America during that time.

Peter Brown and Peter Salem fought along with other Massachusetts men against the large, well-equipped British army at Bunker Hill, the first battle of the war. Jewish patriot Francis Salvador could have been hanged for treason for trying to convince South Carolinians to sign an oath of loyalty to the cause of independence. To protect their children, Abigail and John Adams moved their family out of Boston before the British army arrived. Abigail Adams kept the family farm going and raised her children in the midst of war. John went to Philadelphia to argue for freedom in the Continental Congress. Sixteen-year-old Sybil Ludington risked being captured by British spies when she rode forty miles to rally her father's militia to fight the British. James Armistead, a Virginia slave, could have accepted Britain's promise of freedom by fighting for the English; instead he risked his life, spying for the patriots. Grace Growden Galloway, like other loyalist wives, found herself considered a traitor because her husband had fought for the British. And in 1783, after the last official battle of the war but before the formal peace treaty was signed, Robert Shurtliff answered George Washington's call for recruits to fight roving militias of American loyalists and Mohawks in what we now call New York State.

At the time of the American Revolution, approximately three

million people lived in America. That total included six hundred thousand enslaved Africans and hundreds of thousands of American Indians. People of African descent made up 20 percent of the population. Sixty percent of the white settlers were of English descent, and there were also people of Dutch, Scotch-Irish, German, Portuguese, and Spanish backgrounds. Many of these men, women, and children fought actively for independence. Some sided with the British; some even fought in their army.

American Indians tried to keep out of the struggle, for they saw this conflict as separate from their nations. Eventually, worried about their survival and the loss of more land to white settlers, American Indians found themselves brought into the struggle. Most sided with Great Britain, for they believed the British promises of future trade and the security of their land.

Slaves and freed black men and women served as soldiers, spies, or cooks for both sides. Some white women followed the troops into battle; some fired weapons in certain battles; others took part as caregivers and cooks. Most women stayed home; they spun cloth and sewed uniforms.

You will notice as you read that sometimes we use old-fashioned words such as *Negro* and *colored*, *magazine*, and *commissary*. These words—for African American, a storehouse for arms and ammunition, and an officer in charge of an army's food supplies—were common 250 years ago but are rarely heard today. We feel they evoke the immediacy and reality of life during those times.

Tracking down all the details about the experiences of the Adams family, Francis Salvador, and James Armistead was not possible. We fictionalized some details, based on historical research. In the Acknowledgments section, you can see what has been fictionalized.

We share these stories with you and hope they start you on your own journey to discover other American heroes.

PREPARING FOR WAR

In 1770 many Americans were angry at King George III. They questioned whether laws governing their lives should be made by a king and his lawmakers living three thousand miles away. People in Boston, Massachusetts, hated having four thousand British soldiers in their city. Some Bostonians mocked the British soldiers, calling them "lobsterbacks" because of their red uniforms. They threw snowballs and rocks at them. They gave anti-British speeches in the streets and at meetinghouses. One March day the taunting got out of hand, and British soldiers fired on civilians. Five Americans died. Seven were wounded. The Boston Massacre caused more Americans to question British rule.

Americans were also angry about British taxes, particularly the Stamp Act. Some Americans punished the British agents who tried to collect the tax on printed matter. They tarred and feathered the agents. The Stamp Act was repealed, but new taxes replaced it. In protest more and more colonists stopped buying English goods. On December 16, 1773, angry patriots, disguised as Indians, dumped British tea into Boston's harbor. Furious, the king sent another 2,500 soldiers to keep the Bostonians in order.

When the First Continental Congress met in Philadelphia in June 1774, the delegates argued about how to settle their disagreements with England. Not all Americans or all the delegates were against British rule. Those who favored England called themselves loyalists or Tories. Americans who wanted independence called themselves patriots.

In April 1775 British Lieutenant General Thomas Gage learned that some patriots were storing gunpowder in Massachusetts towns and villages. He sent his troops to Lexington and Concord to seize the powder. The people of Lexington told the British to leave, but they refused. British soldiers fired into the crowd. The attack outraged many Americans. In response ten thousand men left their families and set off for Boston with their local militias to protect New England from the British. They blocked the roads to the city to keep out supplies, hoping this would force the enemy to leave by sea. As the blockade built up, some patriots fled the city, fearing punishment by the British and lack of food.

THE SOLDIER WITH THE PEN:

Peter Brown

In April 1775 the Continental Congress in Philadelphia was still debating whether or not to separate from England. Despite the recent battles at Lexington and Concord, many delegates hoped for a peaceful solution. But even those who were uncertain about independence saw the need for well-equipped, trained troops. On June 15, 1775, the delegates elected George Washington as commander in chief of the Continental army. Before he could get to Boston, the Americans learned that the British planned to fortify the Dorchester Heights peninsula south of Boston in order to control the entrance by sea. They planned to sail across the harbor and attack the American army camped at Cambridge. On the evening of June 16, 1775, the Americans moved first to fortify Bunker Hill across the bay on the Charlestown peninsula.

Peter Brown lifted his pick high off the ground. His arms ached. He had been digging in the dark for almost five hours. How many more rocks were there to move on this steep-sided hill? The twenty-year-old corporal grumbled as he hit more rubble. He stopped to

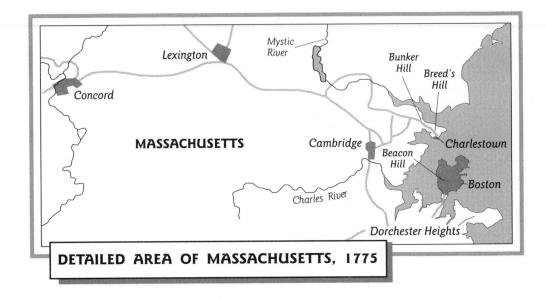

DETAILED AREA OF MASSACHUSETTS, 1775

Lexington

Mystic River

Bunker Hill

Breed's Hill

Concord

MASSACHUSETTS

Cambridge

Beacon Hill

Charlestown

Boston

Charles River

Dorchester Heights

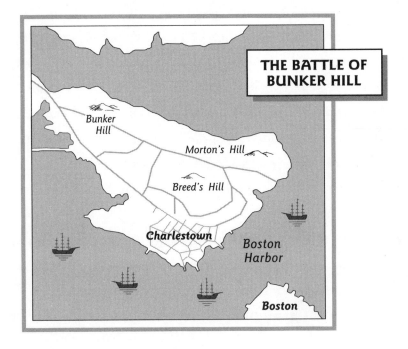

THE BATTLE OF BUNKER HILL

Bunker Hill

Morton's Hill

Breed's Hill

Charlestown

Boston Harbor

Boston

wipe his brow with his bare arm, then swung his pick again.

Like many soldiers here, Brown had fought at Lexington and Concord. He had planned to work this summer in Connecticut but joined the militia instead. He signed on as a corporal to do the duties of clerk and orderly, or messenger. Brown hadn't even had time to write his mother to tell her. If he survived this, he would write her. He touched the quill pen in his pants pocket as if to make the promise.

Since midnight Brown and nine hundred other soldiers in Colonel William Prescott's regiment had chipped away at earth and stone to build a fort on Breed's Hill. Breed's Hill was a perfect place for a fort. It was seventy-five feet high with a wide view of the area around Boston, including the harbor where the British ships were anchored.

The half-completed fort was a rough square. Its 6-foot-high walls were 130 feet long on each side, packed with dirt, wood, and sticks. Brown felt confident that British cannonballs would not be able to penetrate these strong walls.

He was still digging just before sunrise when he heard the booms and crashes of cannonfire from the British ships in the harbor. Obviously a redcoat on watch had spotted the fort. Brown ducked behind the wall. Men digging outside the fort hurried inside and aimed their flintlock muskets. Colonel Prescott shouted to his troops to hold their fire. They were too high up for their muskets to be effective.

The British cannons roared. Brown's ears rang with the sound of the cannonade. The fort trembled, but the few cannonballs that hit high enough on the hill did not penetrate the walls. Still, they did scorch the earth and choke the air with smoke. Brown could hardly breathe. How long would this bombardment last? He waited impatiently until it stopped. When it did, his head still swirled from the terrible noise.

The cannons silent, Colonel Prescott ordered his men back to digging. Make the trenches deeper, he commanded, and pack more earth on the walls. He assigned some soldiers to build wooden platforms for the cannons that would soon arrive from headquarters in Cambridge.

Again Brown chipped away at the earth. It was only five o'clock in the morning, but the day was already unseasonably hot. There wasn't a cloud in the sky. Half an hour passed. The diggers started complaining. They were hungry and thirsty. The operation had been too quickly planned. The men building the platforms demanded to know why the cannons hadn't arrived yet from Cambridge. How could they protect themselves without them?

Prescott ignored their complaints and told them to work harder.

The bombing started again. Brown barely heard Prescott's commands over the roar of the British cannons. In the light of day, he saw that the regiment's only water keg and two kegs of rum lay on the grassy hillside. Before Prescott gave the order to move them

into the fort, a British cannonball hit the water keg. The precious liquid spilled onto the grass. A few soldiers sprang to their feet to bring the rum inside. Several took hearty swigs of the liquor as if it were their last drink.

There was more grumbling as the hours passed.

By eight o'clock the men were still complaining, mostly about their parched throats. A few soldiers volunteered to go down to the village of Charlestown and return with water. Asa Pollard from Billerica, Massachusetts, took the lead, running down the hill. Brown watched in horror as a cannonball exploded near Pollard. Blood coated the grass where Pollard fell. Brown's throat tightened from shock. The young farmer's body was strewn in parts over the grass. Pollard was only fourteen years old. Other soldiers shouted out in response to his hideous death. Some jumped up on the parapet on top of the wall, fixed on Pollard's dead body.

"Get down!" Colonel Prescott ordered.

The British cannons roared again. The men kept shouting, Where are the fresh troops to relieve us?

Scores of men ran for Bunker, the higher hill to the northwest, only five hundred yards away. Brown expected Colonel Prescott to call them back, but he never did. More and more Americans fell wounded on the hill. Prescott shouted at his men to come to order. Some argued defiantly that Asa Pollard deserved a proper burial.

Finally Prescott ordered a grave to be dug. Brown watched the men feverishly dig on the far side of the hill, as far away from the

British cannonballs as they could get.

Then, as if to quiet the troops and show them they had nothing to fear, Prescott scaled the wall. He removed his wig and cocked hat and brandished his sword at the British ships below.

An hour later the troops had calmed down, and Pollard was buried. But the grumbling didn't stop. A few officers approached Prescott. The commander asked Brown to take notes on their conversation.

One officer insisted that the men needed immediate relief. He stressed that they were too tired and hungry to continue. Trying to quiet them, Prescott insisted that the British would not attack the fort.

Out of the corner of his eye, Brown saw men sneaking away to Bunker Hill.

The desertions continued. By ten o'clock Brown counted no more than five hundred men in the fort. Prescott ordered a 330-foot-long wall built to further protect the northeast end of the fort. Make it as high as your chests, he instructed. Peter Brown dug and packed earth under a relentless sun. He tried not to think about the heat or his dry throat. He was one of the lucky ones—at least he had his hat with the large brim to protect him from the sun's glare.

Finally the cannons arrived, pulled by horses. The soldiers immediately protested: Why were there only four cannons? Why had they sent four pounders, the smallest of the big guns? Who was responsible for such a stupid mistake?

A sentry told Prescott soldiers from New Hampshire and Connecticut were building defenses on the beach behind a stone wall and a rail fence. If the British marched across the beach, the Americans would be hidden away, ready to shoot. Brown felt slightly comforted, since he knew the New Hampshire soldiers were extraordinary marksmen.

At noon the British cannons grew silent. Brown looked down and saw why. Twenty-eight big barges were crossing the half-mile distance from Boston to the peninsula. Rows and rows of men in red uniforms were seated in the boats. To protect the redcoat troops, the large British men-of-war anchored in the harbor started firing again at the hill. At one o'clock the British landed.

Brown estimated there were more than two thousand. The redcoats are properly named for their tight crimson waistcoats, he thought. How could they bear those high, stiff collars in this heat? How could they move with sleeves as tight as stockings? Their uniform pants and gaiters up to their calves were just as tight. Brown didn't have a uniform. In fact, none of the Americans but Colonel Prescott had one, and in the heat of the day he had removed his coat.

Brown watched the British strut across the beach. How well-equipped they were with bayonet scabbards, rifles, and muskets. Square cartridge boxes hung on their right hips.

Brown had only a musket. So did most of the other men. Muskets were so clumsy to use. It took sixteen separate motions to load them, and for all that work a musket's shot was inaccurate. You had to aim lower than your mark. You also had to account for the wobble of the lead ball once it left the barrel. Brown had very little ammunition. No American had more than ten rounds of gunpowder and lead.

A third of a mile away, he saw the redcoats walking toward Morton's Hill. Gold glittered on the necks of the officers. The gold crescents, called gorgets, caught the sun's reflection. Their shiny ornaments make perfect targets, Brown thought. Let them climb our hill, the closer the better.

But the British didn't climb. They sat down and took out food from their packs. They were stopping for lunch. How arrogant they are, Brown thought.

In the temporary quiet, Prescott ordered more wounded moved to Bunker Hill. More men than were needed volunteered to do the job. Brown knew they would not return. Prescott said nothing as his men hurriedly took away the wounded.

Brown had no intention of deserting. His gaze was fixed on the redcoats. After lunch they packed up. Straight and strong of step, they began marching confidently up the short hill. Soon they weren't as confident, as many tripped over parts of fences, kilns, and clay pits invisible in the waist-high grass. Walking through swampy patches in the grass slowed them down, too. As they fell upon their comrades, their lines were no longer straight and orderly. Their heavy sacks and weapons made getting up difficult.

Closer, closer. They were marching directly toward the marksmen hidden behind the stone wall on the beach. The crooked first line of redcoats was a hundred or so paces away from them. Suddenly there was a burst of patriot fire. A second burst. A third. Brown had heard the stories about how skillful these New Hampshire men were, but he was still amazed how quickly and accurately they fired.

The four pounders fired, too, and helped push back the British. Then the platform collapsed, and they were quiet.

Brown looked down and cheered as he saw the beach was now strewn with the bodies of British officers. Other soldiers snickered as British soldiers fled in disorder. But Brown knew that didn't mean they were surrendering. It was strangely silent while they regrouped.

A second wave of redcoats started down the beach. This time they walked in columns, ten men deep. When they came into close enough range, the sharpshooters fired. Brown saw blurs of red as British soldiers fell. Now far fewer gorgets caught the sun's reflection.

But the British weren't without their own strategy, he saw. Some redcoats had changed direction. They turned to climb Breed's Hill from the southeast, digging heels into the sloped earth for better footing.

Prescott moved about the fort, urging his men not to shoot until the enemy was closer. When the British were sixty yards away, he gave the order to fire, but their musket balls and powder could not reach the enemy.

"Hold your fire!" he shouted.

Perspiration tingled in Brown's pores. The enemy was now only twenty yards away.

"Fire!" William Prescott bellowed.

From every direction, powder exploded and lead blasted upon the British. They scrambled down the hill. Some fired back as they ran. Brown heard moaning and shouting about him as British soldiers hit their targets. Through the smoke and dust, he saw more men in his regiment fleeing for the safety of Bunker Hill. Then suddenly from the south, the sky was red with leaping flames. The British men-of-war had a new target! They were bombing the village of Charlestown. The church steeple was a pyramid of fire, and buildings fell together in ruins.

"Only one round left." William Prescott's shirt was covered in dust like the rest of his soldiers.

The Americans readied for a third British advance. They gathered twigs, rocks, and pieces of glass to use as gunshot. Peter Brown did a quick head count. Only 150 men were left in the fort. Some were too wounded to fight. Yet he took heart. Twice they had repelled the mighty British army. Surely they could do it a third time.

Below, two more British regiments marched along the beach. The marksmen hit the soldiers in the front. A column of redcoats started climbing the hill from the southeast. A third group ascended from the southwest side. Now they were moving quickly, for they had thrown off their waistcoats and packs and carried only bayonets. Brown saw their fourteen-inch blades raised to attack.

He ripped the cartridge paper with his teeth and poured powder into his musket. He heard the lead ball plunk down with it. Then he fired his last round of ammunition. The enemy fell back temporarily as more Americans hit their targets.

Another wave of redcoats started marching toward the fort. The smoke around them made it hard to see where to fire. Brown loaded his musket with twigs. The man next to him stuffed rocks and dirt into his.

The British were close, mere feet away. Now they were in the trench. In a minute they would climb over the fort walls.

Brown noticed Peter Salem, a free Negro from Framingham, raising his gun to shoot. Through air that was clouded from cannon fire, gunshot, and blood, Brown followed the line of Salem's aim to British Major Pitcairn. It was Pitcairn's men who had opened fire upon the people at Lexington. With his last bit of lead and powder, Peter Salem felled Major John Pitcairn.

The British stormed over the parapet and from the rear of the fort, pointing their bayonets at everyone in their path. Brown struck out with the butt of his musket. Others used rocks and their fists. But there were too many redcoats. They couldn't keep them off the wall or push them back into the trench.

"Retreat!" ordered William Prescott.

There was a flurry of feet and hands as his men scrambled

through the opening in the fort and down the north side of Breed's Hill. The soldiers who had deserted on Bunker Hill ran to join them. Brown did not look back at the fort, but he knew not everyone had gotten away. Some were trapped by the enemy's bayonets.

It was hard not tripping over the powder horns, water bottles, sacks, and bloodied British bodies that were nearly invisible in the high grass. The sharpshooters on the beach provided cover as they struggled to hurdle stone walls.

The two-and-a-half-hour battle was over. William Prescott led his men back to the camp in Cambridge. The British had taken Breed's Hill, but Peter Brown was not alone in feeling that they had won a victory. Their small, untrained volunteer army had shown the British that they were willing to fight.

Eight days later Peter Brown wrote to his mother about the battle: "Oh, may I never forget God's distinguishing mercy to me in sparing my life. If we should ever be called again to action, I hope to have courage and the strength to act my part."

This battle on June 17, 1775, was recorded in the historical records as the Battle of Bunker Hill. The reasons were twofold. First, the defensive plan had been to fortify Bunker Hill. Upon arriving there, Prescott's officers suggested that Breed's Hill was preferable, because it was closer to Boston than Bunker and the American light cannons could not reach the city or harbor from as high as the top of the taller Bunker Hill. A second reason was that most of the Americans spent the battle on Bunker Hill.

When they returned home, they told stories of how they "fought" on Bunker. Very few mentioned that the action really took place on Breed's Hill. Those who had deserted to Bunker Hill did not tell their families.

Peter Brown's letter to his mother was one of the most detailed eyewitness records of the Battle of Bunker Hill. Brown, along with Peter Salem, fought with the Continental army until the war ended.

While the patriots did not stop the British from taking the peninsula of Charlestown, they killed and wounded more than 1,000 British soldiers. The British lost 40 percent of their men to death or injury, including officers. More than 150 American soldiers died, and nearly 300 Americans were wounded or captured.

After this battle many more Americans favored independence. They were proud of how their soldiers had stood up to the mighty British army.

Two weeks later, on July 2, 1775, George Washington arrived in Cambridge to lead the Continental army. The colonies moved one step closer to war with England.

THE OATH:
Francis Salvador

Patriots and loyalists actively campaigned to win over their neighbors to their ways of thinking. In the backcountry of South Carolina, both groups had militias. South Carolina's patriots held meetings to win converts to the cause of independence and to get them to swear an oath of loyalty. Anyone who signed the oath vowed to support the cause of independence and the decisions of the Continental Congress. The British considered signing the oath an act of treason, punishable by death.

Francis Salvador pulled his horse to a halt at Fort Boone. The pastureland was lush and green this late August afternoon of 1775. He admired the powerful flow of Long Cane Creek just beyond the preaching shed. Long Cane Creek was much higher than the creeks near his plantation forty miles east. Numerous horses and wagons spotted the adjacent field. He was pleased by the size of the crowd this morning.

Dismounting, he nodded his approval to his travel companion,

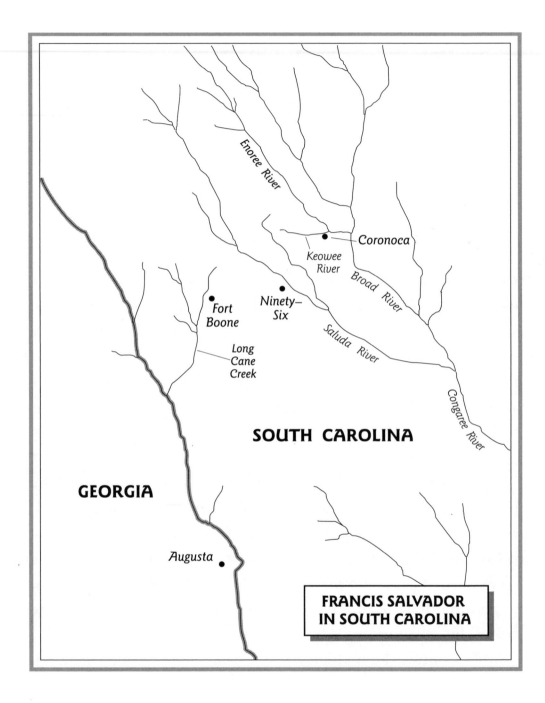

Enoree River

Coronoca

Keowee
River

Broad River

Fort
Boone

Ninety–
Six

Saluda River

Long
Cane
Creek

Congaree River

SOUTH CAROLINA

GEORGIA

Augusta

**FRANCIS SALVADOR
IN SOUTH CAROLINA**

William Tennent. Over recent weeks, they had visited many settlements like Fort Boone, trying to get signatures for the oath of loyalty.

They tethered their horses around the trunk of a giant chestnut tree. Salvador took a leather case from his saddlebag. It contained the all-important oath. He watched Tennent walk toward the shed, his Bible in hand. His friend was ready to deliver his sermon.

The two men had ridden twelve miles since early morning after an uncomfortable night's sleep on the broken clay floor of a kindly farmer's house. How different was this South Carolina wilderness from Salvador's home in London! Two years ago, at his uncle's suggestion, the twenty-eight-year-old nobleman had left his wife and four children in England to come here and save what was left of the family fortune.

It had been a wise decision. The family plantation was rich land. Some of his neighbors called his 1,790 acres at Coronoca "Corn-acre" after the region's most plentiful crop. This year's corn and indigo looked to be even better than last year's. But what good would bumper crops be if England decided to tax them?

Today's meeting was not going to be easy. Most farmers in this part of South Carolina were poor and dependent on selling their crops to England. Signing the oath meant you agreed to stop trading with England. These farmers didn't like the English Parliament telling them what to do, and they weren't sure they wanted the Continental Congress making decisions for them either.

Salvador found a seat at the back of the shed and looked about at mostly unfamiliar faces. He was relieved to see very few guns. At last week's meeting on the Enoree River, loyalist Colonel Thomas Fletchall and three men from his militia had stood with pointed pistols throughout the meeting. The guns had scared almost everyone from signing the oath.

The backcountry farmers dressed like Salvador did, in leather jerkins and homespun shirts. Soon after arriving in South Carolina, he had put away his velvet suits, powdered wigs, and low-cut shoes with silver buckles.

Although he was wealthier than most of these men, he had much in common with them. Many farmers were Scotch-Irish Presbyterians. They had been forced by King James I to emigrate from Scotland to Northern Ireland. Prejudice followed them there, so they moved to the New World, hoping for a fresh start.

Like these farmers, Salvador was no stranger to religious persecution. He was a Jew. Three hundred years ago, his people had been expelled from Portugal. His family resettled in Holland. The shadow of anti-Semitism eventually surfaced there, so the family moved to England. They found prejudice in England, too. His uncle, Joseph Salvador, had brought a delegation of wealthy Portuguese Jews to King George III to pay their respects when he took the throne. Afterward, when Joseph Salvador pressed for a law to make Portuguese Jews naturalized citizens of England, he was booed in a theater and forced to leave. The bill never passed Parliament. Now his nephew was dedicated to freedom in South Carolina.

Standing at the front of the shed, Reverend William Tennent opened his Bible and called the meeting to order. His voice boomed: "'I said to the king, "May the king live forever!"'" The loyalists cheered his words honoring a king. Salvador waited to hear what would come next. He was unfamiliar with these words from the Old Testament, but he knew that his friend had no intention of praising royalty.

Tennent invoked the Bible whenever he spoke. It helped soften people and win them over to his viewpoint. The reverend continued, "'Why should my face not be sad, when the city, the place of my ancestors' graves, lies waste, and its gates have been destroyed by fire?'" The city was Jerusalem. He was trying to help the audience understand that South Carolina, like Jerusalem, was ruled by an outsider who cared little for their wishes. Salvador appreciated the reverend's style and zeal. No matter how many times he heard him speak, he was always affected by his fiery voice.

"Long live King George III!" someone shouted.

Other loyalists echoed the sentiment.

"Down with unfair taxation without representation," countered a patriot.

"What does King George know of our life here?" yelled another.

"Traitor!"

"Redcoat lover!"

In the past month Salvador had heard these accusations over

and over again in the backcountry.

William Tennent shouted for order. "In the words of the Continental Congress in Philadelphia," he bellowed, "we will not import goods from England into British America."

"There is no British America," a patriot shouted.

"That's what you say," a loyalist yelled.

Tennent continued as though he did not hear the shouts and the booing and clapping that followed. "Starting in two weeks, we will not export or import anything to or from Great Britain or Ireland. We will still export rice to Europe."

"How are we supposed to support our families if we can't sell our goods?"

Francis Salvador stood. "If we continue to feed England, how can we force King George to recognize our demands?"

"Here. Here. Down with exports!"

"Easy for a cattle trader to say. You'll get by. But we farmers won't."

John Harris, the minister of the Long Cane Creek area, stepped up to the front of the shed and took over. "The gospel according to Mark," he began. "'Listen! A sower went out to sow.'"

The crowd grew quiet, for they knew this familiar passage from the New Testament.

"'And as he sowed,'" Harris continued, "'some seed fell on the path, and the birds came and ate it up. Other seed fell on rocky ground, where it did not have much soil. And when the sun rose, it

was scorched. Other seed fell among thorns, and choked. Other seed fell into good soil and brought forth grain.'"

Harris explained his words in simple, clear language: "The good soil is each farmer who sows seeds of justice in his fields. When you step forward to sign the oath of loyalty, you, too, will share in the ideals of the kingdom of heaven while on earth." His words quieted even the opposition.

John Harris grabbed the moment. "Mr. Salvador, bring the oath forward."

But before Salvador could get to the front of the shed, someone yelled, "If we sign, how will you help us protect ourselves against the loyalist militia?"

"Our militia doesn't have enough gunpowder to fight," another patriot added.

"By the authority of the Provincial Congress of South Carolina," Tennent said, "I promise to get you gunpowder." He lowered his voice and leaned toward the audience. "But now I make the motion that it is time to sign the oath," he said.

"I second the motion," shouted Harris.

"I second it, too," said Salvador.

More shouting. Loyalists and patriots alike accused one another of wanting to solve their differences with guns. People called out the names of friends who had been threatened with guns to change their minds about independence. They shouted about the brutality of the other side.

Harris ignored the shouting and nodded toward Francis Salvador. Salvador opened his case on the small wooden table below the platform where William Tennent and John Harris were standing. He removed his quill pen and inkwell and put them on the table. Next to them, he placed the oath of loyalty.

Salvador heard grumbling among the loyalists. He looked up and saw a long line of men coming forward to sign. The patriots had won the argument today. His uncle would be proud.

Clashes between loyalists and patriots in the backcountry continued as the colonists moved toward independence. The British tried to win the Cherokees in South Carolina over to their side. They pointed out that American colonists had broken treaties and built frontier settlements on Cherokee land. In May 1776 the Cherokees began the first of many devastating attacks on South Carolina frontier settlements. On July 31, 1776, as a diversion while the British attempted to take Charlestown (currently Charleston), loyalists and Cherokees fought the patriot militia in nearby Ninety Six District. Twenty-nine-year-old Francis Salvador was killed during this battle.

Outnumbered, the patriots at Ninety Six were forced to retreat. They regrouped. Helped by militias from North Carolina and Virginia, they raided and devastated Cherokee settlements over the late summer and early fall. On October 11, 1776, the Cherokees agreed to sign a treaty, giving up a large part of their territory.

South Carolina's patriots did not forget Francis Salvador. As mentioned in Abraham J. Karp's The Jewish Experience in America, *William Henry Drayton, chief justice of the South Carolina Supreme Court, wrote of his friend, "The fate of this gentleman excited universal regret. His manners were those of a polished gentleman. As such, he was intimately known and esteemed by the first revolutionary characters in South Carolina."*

"YOURS, PORTIA":
Abigail Adams

Abigail and John Adams were ardent patriots. They lived on Queen Street in Boston with their four children until the tension in the city between patriots and loyalists made it too dangerous for them to be there. They feared that John might be arrested as a traitor, for the British knew how strongly he supported independence. To safeguard the children, the family moved in June 1774 to their farm in Braintree, ten miles southeast of Boston.

In September John left Braintree for Philadelphia to be a delegate to the Continental Congress. Abigail and the children stayed on the farm.

In July 1775 George Washington set up camp at Cambridge, across the river from Boston, hoping to force the British to leave the city. Months passed, but the British were still in control of Boston. Abigail and her children tried to get used to life without John. Nearing Christmas, they were especially lonely for him.

Eight-year-old John Quincy, known as Johnny, warmed his hands before the fireplace. It was a cold night, this twenty-first of

December 1775, but the parlor fire took away some of the chill. Johnny turned to his audience. "Ready?" he shouted to his brothers, sister, and cousin.

Abigail Adams looked up from her desk and watched the children quickly come to attention.

"Ready!" Johnny pretended to shoulder a musket.

Abigail knew what was coming. This afternoon Johnny had seen the militia drill outside the Braintree meetinghouse.

He moved the gun to position. He bit off the end of the make-believe cartridge paper and put powder into the gun's pan. Standing the musket on its fat end, he dropped the remaining powder, ball, and rolled-up paper into the barrel. With an invisible ramrod, he pushed it down. He raised the gun, held it level with the ground, and pulled back the flints. "Fire!" He pulled the trigger, and the children cheered the imaginary explosion and the pretend ball flying from the muzzle.

Johnny took his bows. Just as Abigail was about to remind them that it was time to go to bed, Johnny repeated his pantomime. She looked down at her ledger. She had to get the children upstairs soon. There was work to do. With John away, she was in charge of the farm and the family's finances. Everything cost much more since the British occupied Boston.

Still, her family was more comfortable than so many others. They had ample food and money. Their apple orchard provided plenty of cider. They had grain and healthy livestock. But they were

not immune to illness. Two months ago, everyone in the household came down with dysentery. Abigail's servant girl died. She and the children had survived the diarrhea, vomiting, and fevers of this terrible disease. Her mother and John's youngest brother, Elihu, had not.

She glanced away from Johnny to her husband's last letter on top of the pile of bills. She must write John tonight. Abigail knew he was as lonely for her as she was for him. She had seen him only twice this year, on short visits in March and August. Letters traveled slowly to Philadelphia. She hoped he had received her correspondence from two weeks ago. She so wanted him to have a cheerful greeting for Christmas.

The whinnying of horses stopped Johnny's performance. Someone was coming—maybe neighbors with news. Hopefully not more local militiamen, rushing off to Boston.

Everyone in the parlor paused to listen. Abigail stared at the closed front door. Now the whinnying sounded familiar.

"Hurry, children."

They rushed to the door. John held out his arms to embrace his wife.

"Your letter said you weren't coming home," she said.

"I was given leave to visit my dear family. You're not disappointed, are you?" John answered jokingly.

He opened his embrace to make room for their four children and niece Susanna. Nabby was ten, Johnny and Susanna were eight, Charley was five, and Tommy was four. Susanna was the daughter of John's youngest brother, who had died. The children herded their father into the parlor, shouting questions over one another.

John asked for quiet. He told them his important news. He had been appointed chief justice of the Massachusetts Superior Court. Before he could explain what the job meant, Tommy blurted out, "Is the battle finished?"

Abigail suppressed a smile. No matter how many times she told Tommy otherwise, he still believed that Papa was a soldier in battle. For Tommy, being a soldier was the only possible reason for his father to be away.

"No, son, the battle is not finished."

"Did you receive my last letter?" asked Nabby.

"Yes," John replied. "And I'm so proud that you are learning Latin and French."

"Did you bring any books about kings and queens?" asked Charley. His father answered that he would send them books when he returned to Philadelphia.

Even with a revolution going on, the children are still taken with royalty, Abigail mused.

His father congratulated Johnny again, this time on his studies. Then, without waiting to be asked, Johnny picked up a book from the table and began to read from *The Histories* by Polybius, written in the second century B.C. in ancient Rome.

Johnny loved the story of the eighteen-year-old Roman hero, Scipio Africanus. During battle against Hannibal and his army, Scipio's father fell from his horse, and the enemy surrounded him. His bodyguards made no move to help him. Then Scipio Africanus charged into the battle on horseback, and the bodyguards spurred their horses and galloped after the young warrior. They encircled Scipio's father and saved his life.

In a loud, confident voice, Johnny kept reading.

"It's late, Johnny," Abigail interrupted.

Despite the children's protests, she and John put them to bed. Each in turn asked John if he would be there in the morning. He assured them that he would be.

The house was quiet again. John and Abigail settled in before the parlor fire. He told her about the latest events in Philadelphia: The delegates in Congress were still split about independence. King George III had offered to pardon any colony that gave up the struggle for independence. The loyalists were working hard to convince the uncommitted delegates to vote for peace instead of revolution. John was worried the loyalists might win. He expressed his concern over another matter, too. Should he stay a delegate to the Congress or accept the appointment as chief justice and remain home?

"You know I consider you my home-front reporter," he said.

How easy it would be to tell him to stay home, and how wonderful it would be to have him here. Abigail missed him terribly, but she knew that John's clear voice for the country's independence was needed in Philadelphia. She would listen as always to his thoughts, but she would not choose for him.

"It's your decision, I would think," she answered.

John urged her to come back with him to Philadelphia. Many delegates' wives had moved there, and he longed for the daily comfort of having her at his side. Abigail's look told him she had not changed her mind about leaving the children with relatives. She had argued in the past that she would not have them be without a father *and* a mother. Besides, if she went to Philadelphia, who would run the farm? His salary as a delegate could not support them.

A month later, John left for Philadelphia. The British remained in control of Boston. Abigail and her children stayed on in Braintree.

On the evening of March 2, Abigail heard cannon fire. George Washington's campaign to roust the British from Boston had begun. The battle raged for fifteen days. On March 17 Abigail and the children joyously watched the white masts of the British fleet make their way out to the Atlantic Ocean toward New York.

Once again Boston belonged to the patriots. Church bells rang. The gates of the newly liberated city were reopened, and Washington led the triumphant American army inside. Boston's patriots fell into line after the soldiers. Children rushed to touch

Washington's coattails.

But Abigail's Boston was a mess. Before leaving, the British had poured molasses and salt onto the cobblestone streets to make it difficult for people to walk and for horses to pull carriages. They carried off linens, wool, and small valuables. What they could not carry in their packs, they threw into the harbor. The tides brought remnants of feather beds and broken china to Braintree.

Patriots who had fled the city started moving back. Abigail wanted to go to her home on Queen Street immediately, but she didn't dare. Smallpox was raging in Boston. She couldn't risk bringing sickness back to the children. A friend in town checked on the house. He reported that it was dirty, but there was no real damage from the British army doctor who had occupied it.

The new peace felt delicious. The family was safe. It was spring. Birds fluttered in the warming sun. It was time to prepare the fields for planting. She had to find time to answer John's recent letters, too. He had written that the delegates were struggling over the document announcing independence from Britain.

Abigail wanted independence to be declared. American women needed independence. They had so few rights. Once women married, their husbands owned their money and property. They couldn't even leave their jewelry or clothing to their children without their husband's approval. In the case of divorce, husbands were automatically given custody of the children. Although Abigail had run the farm for two years and paid the family's bills, she could not sign a business contract. John knew all of this as well as she did, and yet she had heard nothing from him about it. It was time for the home-front reporter to remind him.

> *March 31, 1776*
> *Dearest Friend,*
> *I long to hear that you have declared an independency. And, by the way, in the new Code of Laws, I desire you would Remember the Ladies, and be more generous and favorable to them than your ancestors. Do not put such unlimited power into the hands of the husbands. Remember, all men would be tyrants if they could. If particular care and attention is not paid to the ladies, we are determined to foment a rebellion. We will not hold ourselves bound by any laws in which we have no voice or representation.*
> *Yours, Portia*

Portia was the wife of the Roman statesman Brutus. Abigail used the name often when writing to John, for he, too, was a statesman in the service of his country, and she was a statesman's wife.

Fifteen days later John responded to Abigail's suggestion to "Remember the Ladies":

> *As to your extraordinary Code of Laws, I cannot but laugh. Depend on it, we know better than to repeal our masculine*

systems. Although they are in full force, you know they are little more than theory. We dare not exert our power in its full latitude. We are obliged to go fair, and softly, and in practice you know we are the subjects. We have only the name of masters. And, rather than give up this, which would completely subject us to the despotism of the petticoat, I hope General Washington and all our brave heroes would fight.

Abigail did not find John's response amusing. How dare he make a joke of women's independence by saying that women with rights would become tyrants. Ha! Despotism of the petticoat, indeed! He obviously needed more education to understand why equality was as essential for women as it was for men. She wrote:

I cannot say that I think you very generous to the Ladies, for while you are proclaiming peace and goodwill to Men, emancipating all nations, you insist upon absolute power over wives. But you must remember that arbitrary power is like most other things, which are very hard, and very liable to be broken. Notwithstanding all your wise laws, we have it in our power not only to free ourselves, but to subdue our masters, and, without violence, throw your authority at our feet.

Yours, Portia

Without one dissenting vote, John and the other delegates to the Second Continental Congress signed the Declaration of Independence on July 4, 1776. Abigail's concerns about women's equality were never addressed in the Declaration or in the Constitution.

For most of the next eight years, many more miles lay between Abigail and John, as he attended to the concerns of the new nation. In all, they wrote more than twelve hundred letters to each other. Their son John Quincy Adams also became an avid letter writer, writing not only to his father but to other statesmen.

Finally, in June 1784, Abigail and John were reunited in France, where John had negotiated the peace treaty between the United States and Great Britain. In 1796 John Adams was elected the second president of the United States. Abigail Adams died on October 28, 1818. John lived to see their son "Johnny" become the sixth president of the United States in 1825. John Adams died on July 4, 1826, the same day as Thomas Jefferson.

Seventy-two years after the Declaration of Independence was signed, on July 19 and 20, 1848, a public meeting in Seneca Falls, New York, launched a women's rights movement. As Abigail Adams had predicted, American women fomented a rebellion to gain equality. It took another seventy-two years, until 1920, for them to win the right to vote.

THE DECISION:
George Washington

It was Christmas Eve, 1776. George Washington had a desperate situation on his hands. Since forcing the British out of Boston last March, the Continental army had suffered one humiliation after another. Four months ago, they had lost Long Island. They had retreated from the city of New York in September and from White Plains in October. For the past two months, Washington had kept his army on the move. His soldiers were ill from dysentery, pneumonia, and yellow jaundice. Some were deserting.

Most soldiers were due to return home after the New Year. Washington knew his men needed a victory to convince them to re-enlist.

The British army was spending the winter in New York. Hessian soldiers, hired out by their German lords to fight for the British, were not as lucky. They had been ordered to stay in New Jersey to protect the outpost line along the Delaware River.

Twilight was giving way to darkness on Christmas Eve, 1776, as General George Washington's officers ate cold meat and sipped

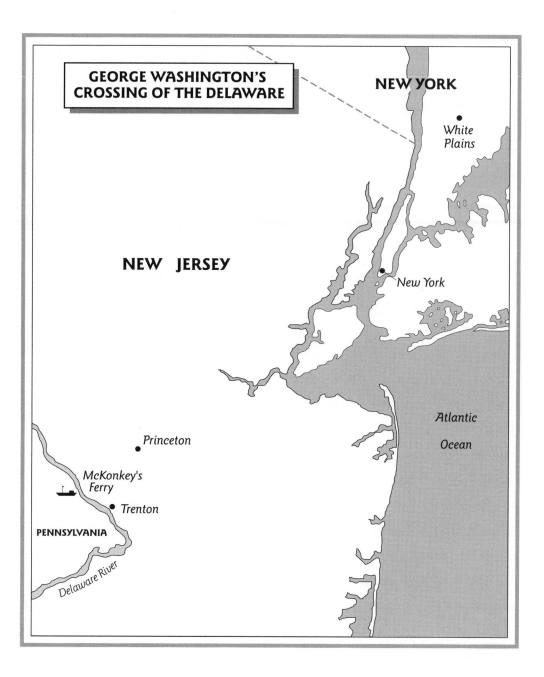

GEORGE WASHINGTON'S CROSSING OF THE DELAWARE

NEW YORK

White Plains

NEW JERSEY

New York

Princeton

McKonkey's Ferry

Trenton

PENNSYLVANIA

Delaware River

Atlantic Ocean

small beer. Brewed with hops, the beer was weaker than ale, but they were glad to have it.

When the food was cleared away, the lanky, forty-three-year-old Virginian rose to speak. He explained that he had made what might be his most important, yet troubling, decision so far. He hoped this decision would turn the tide of the war toward the patriots. Late in the afternoon tomorrow, on Christmas Day, the army would cross the Delaware River from Pennsylvania into New Jersey. They would march under cover of darkness and attack the Hessian soldiers in Trenton. The Hessians would undoubtedly be celebrating Christmas and be caught off guard by the attack.

The plan was simple. Washington had divided the troops into three groups. He would lead 2,400 men across the river near McKonkey's Ferry, Pennsylvania, landing nine miles north of Trenton. A second division of 1,000 men, led by General James Ewing, would cross the Delaware a mile south of Trenton and seize the bridge over the Assunpink Creek. Colonel John Cadwalader would lead a third group of 1,000 soldiers. His men would cross twenty miles downstream at Bristol and attack the Hessian outpost there. That action would be a diversion from the main attack and keep the Hessians in Bristol too busy to go to Trenton.

Every officer in the room knew that the Hessians, under the command of Colonel Johann Gottlieb Rall, were fierce, highly disciplined soldiers. It would be a major success to defeat them. A victory might just convince the Continental army that this war could be won.

After Washington spoke, he waited for his officers to comment. Not one man spoke of the possible consequences of a failed attack. No one said how dangerous the plan was, although everyone knew there were loyalist spies all over New Jersey who might warn Rall. If that happened, Rall's men would be waiting with their rifles on the other side of the river.

Washington stood at the edge of the Delaware River at McKonkey's Ferry. He pulled his thick wool cloak around him as tightly as possible. It was impossible to stay warm, even properly dressed as he was. How must his men feel, wearing the thinnest of coats and shirts and pants? Many had rags around their feet instead of shoes. Still others were barefoot. Some wore broken shoes; the snow beneath their feet was tinged with blood. Although their feet and hands were almost frostbitten, not one man murmured a complaint.

No one could tell Washington that Americans were not courageous. These farmers, carpenters, blacksmiths, merchants, and fishermen were giving all they had to fight for their country under unbearable circumstances. He was asking them to do the near impossible, and they were doing it. He prayed that he had made the right decision.

He listened as one of his officers quoted Thomas Paine. He hoped Paine's fiery eloquence would rally his men. "'These are times that try men's souls,'" the officer read. "'The summer soldier and the sunshine patriot will, in this crisis, shrink from the service of their country, but he that stands it now deserves the love and thanks of man and woman. The harder the conflict, the more glorious the triumph.'"

The troops lined up silently to cross the river. Eight hundred feet of water separated Pennsylvania from New Jersey. Today the river was choked with ice. The morning had been cold but sunny. By noon the temperature rose into the thirties. Then a cold front moved in. There were ice floes everywhere. Washington worried that the ice might thicken even more. If it thickened too much, the boats would not be able to move. His only hope of getting the army across was Colonel John Glover's regiment.

Glover's regiment was unusual for the times: It consisted of free Negro and white fishermen and sailors from Marblehead, Massachusetts. Most of the white soldiers in the army had never seen Negroes work as their equals. Many didn't like the idea, and some hated it. Washington greatly respected Glover's soldiers. They had proved their extraordinary skill this past August when the British had the rebels hemmed in on Brooklyn Heights. Through a dense fog and rain, they had ferried 9,500 men, horses, cannons, and supplies across Long Island Sound to escape. If humanly possible, they would not fail him now.

"Move on." Colonel Henry Knox's deep bass voice boomed as he tried to hurry the men into the boats. Knox was in charge of artillery, which amounted to only eighteen cannons. The 2,400 soldiers would cross first, then the two hundred horses, and finally the eighteen big guns.

The best boats for crossing were the Durham boats. These black boats were forty to sixty feet long with slightly pointed ends. They were designed to haul heavy loads of pig iron. Washington watched Glover's men push away from the Pennsylvania shore. The snow was falling more densely now, and it was almost impossible to see the boats. But still Washington tried to follow their movement across to New Jersey, then back to Pennsylvania, then across to New Jersey again.

After an hour Knox told Washington there were enough men on the New Jersey side to provide protection. He could cross now. He stepped into a boat. General Nathanael Greene followed at his heels. Greene was a Quaker. His people were pacifists: They did not take up arms. But Greene believed so strongly in independence that he had joined the army.

The boat rocked as other men stepped into it. Ice banged at the sides of the boat as it slid away from the shore. General William Blackler's muscular arms fought the swift current. He alternated— oars, pole, oars, pole. The ice crunched against the hull as the boat lurched slowly forward.

The vicious wind bit Washington's cheeks and burned his eyes. He could not see through the blinding snow to New Jersey, but Blackler seemed to instinctively know where it was. Oars, pole . . . The ice banged and banged against the sides of the boat. Sleet drenched Washington's cloak through to his cotton shirt. The wet cotton irritated his skin, which burned and felt frozen at the same time.

How far across were they? Had they made any progress at all in these swollen waters? Suddenly the boat bumped against land. Two officers grabbed at the snowy riverbank.

It took several minutes to steady the boat, for even at the shoreline the current was strong. Washington stepped onto New Jersey soil. The few hundred soldiers who had already crossed were standing or sitting on the snow. There was no enemy in sight. It was eight o'clock. He had calculated that the whole army would cross by midnight. It was clear now that it would be closer to three or four in the morning. Then they would have to march nine miles to Trenton; it would be daylight when they arrived. There were Tory sympathizers living all along the route. Would they warn Rall that the enemy was coming? He pushed the disturbing thought away. The risk had to be taken.

Washington pulled his wet cloak about him and, through sleet and freezing rain, watched the blur of boats going back and forth. From Pennsylvania to New Jersey, back to Pennsylvania, then across to New Jersey. Sit down, his officers urged. He refused. He had no right to comfort when his men stood without shoes, soaked from head to toe.

An hour passed. A second hour. Someone brought over a wooden box and persuaded Washington to finish his vigil on it. It was not until three in the morning that men, horses, and cannons had crossed.

Washington despaired. His plan to surprise the Hessians by midnight had gone afoul. Were Ewing's and Cadwalader's men across by now? There was no way of knowing, and no turning back. He had to push on.

Three scouts rode ahead. There was no one on the road. But then, who would be out on such a night? There had to be some advantage to this terrible weather.

The snow soon combined with hail. The frozen pellets whipped at Washington's back. He felt as though he were being cut by a knife. How could his men endure this in their ragged shirts? Soldiers with bare feet slid on the ice. They struggled to get up. He ordered his officers to march alongside the men and encourage them.

"Victory or death! Victory or death!" the officers repeated. Washington hoped these words reminded his men of the alternative to success.

When they reached the tiny hamlet of Birmingham, the army separated into two groups. Washington led half the men along the northern road to Trenton. Nathanael Greene went with him. General John Sullivan and Colonel John Stark took the rest of the troops by the southern route.

They marched against battering snow and sleet. No one spoke a word. The wheels of the carriages lugging the cannons dug deep grooves into the snow. Again men slipped and fell. Their comrades helped them up, often falling back down with them. Others dragged them to their feet, for everyone knew that if you didn't get up immediately, you might fall asleep and freeze to death.

"Soldiers, keep by your officers," Washington urged. His horse lost footing. He seized the mane just in time for the animal to recover.

Sunrise found them a mile outside Trenton. Suddenly there was a flurry of movement in the woods. Was it Hessian soldiers? Keep marching but be ready to attack, General Greene ordered. His men trudged on. Twenty American soldiers appeared from behind a string of pine trees.

"State who you are," Greene demanded.

"Soldiers from the Fifth Virginia Regiment led by Captain Richard Clough Anderson." The spokesman explained that they were scouting for enemy outposts. There was pride in his voice when he said that they had killed six Hessians.

Washington was infuriated. "You may have ruined my plans for keeping the Hessians off guard," he snapped. It took him a few minutes to regain his composure. Then he told the men of the Fifth Virginia Regiment to fall in with his troops.

At eight o'clock in the morning, Washington's troops reached the northern outskirts of Trenton. He knew somewhere close were Hessian soldiers on guard duty. They had to be captured so Rall could not be warned. But where were they? He had to find out. A lone man was chopping wood outside his house. Washington had

to take a chance that this man was *not* a loyalist. "Can you tell me where the Hessian picket is?" he asked.

The man hesitated.

"You need not be frightened," said one of Washington's aides. "General George Washington is asking the question."

The man pointed to a house on the left side of the road.

But before Washington could give any orders, a Hessian ran out of the house firing his musket. A second man ran out firing, then a third. From behind trees and fences, Washington's men fired back.

There was a boom of cannons from the west and south. Then another thunder of explosions. Then the sound of musket fire. The army was attacking Trenton. His plan was working.

Within minutes Washington received reports of the battle: The cannons had awakened the Hessians. They were running out in the streets, pulling up their pants and boots and firing wildly through the blinding snow. They ran in all directions, trying to get away. But they couldn't. The Americans were everywhere.

American soldiers suddenly appeared in one street and then reappeared in another street. They ran through the blinding snow, shouting and firing at the Hessians, their bayonets poised to attack. Those who had swords were swinging them at everyone in their paths. It was as Washington had known it would be. His men weren't afraid of anything.

As the battle continued, Washington received more updates: The cannons had worked their damage. But despite cannon and musket fire all about them, a few Hessian soldiers reached the two cannons in front of Colonel Rall's headquarters. They got off two shots, then hitched the horses to the cannons to move the big guns up the icy street. Rebel fire downed them.

Colonel Rall mounted his horse and rallied his men to battle. "Be calm," he commanded as they fell into line behind him. "Fix your bayonets," he shouted. Three hundred strong, they marched down the street into the thick of the enemies' fire. A ball from a musket of a Pennsylvania soldier hit its mark, and Rall was wounded. Rall's soldiers carried him away from the battle.

His leaderless men refused to surrender. They marched two deep in a straight line, down the main street on their own counterattack. In the swirl of icy rain, it was impossible to see them. The Americans waited patiently until they were within two hundred yards. Then they ran toward them, muskets in hand, though most knew that their wet gunpowder would never fire. The Hessians fired back; their wet weapons did not work either. They tried reloading, but by that time the Americans were all over them, swinging their muskets and fists.

Within ninety minutes the musket and cannon fire came to a halt and Washington received the news that Rall wanted to surrender. When the dying commander presented Washington with his sword, the American general promised to treat Rall's captured soldiers with honor.

Washington called his officers together, expressing his pride in the courage and resourcefulness of their men. He couldn't have been more pleased to hear the statistics. The Continental army had captured 868 Hessians, six cannons, a thousand muskets, forty gallons of rum, and the musical instruments of Colonel Rall's band. Twenty-two Hessians were dead. Ninety-eight were wounded. No one was yet certain how many Americans were killed, but it was believed to be very few.

Unfortunately at least five hundred Hessian soldiers had escaped via Assunpink Creek. General Ewing's men were not there to stop them. His troops had not been able to cross the Delaware. Cadwalader's men had managed to cross the river but returned to Pennsylvania when they couldn't get their cannons across. Washington was perplexed why neither group had been successful, but he said nothing.

He asked his officers: Should they march north to Princeton and surprise the Hessian forces there, or should they return to Pennsylvania with their prisoners? Greene and Knox pressed to go ahead, but the other officers were against it. The weather was still brutal. The men were exhausted and wet. Many had drunk too much of the captured rum.

Washington decided the army would return to Pennsylvania.

As Washington had hoped, the victory at Trenton boosted morale. More than 1,400 American men agreed to re-enlist in the Continental army for an additional six weeks. They were joined by 3,600 recruits from volunteer militias in Pennsylvania.

On January 3, Washington led his troops in a successful attack on Princeton. In three short weeks, the Continental army had retaken New Jersey. The Continental army could rest now for the remainder of the winter while their commander in chief planned his strategy.

TARNATION SYBIL!:
Sybil Ludington

The victories in Trenton and Princeton boosted morale, but the war was far from over. By the early months of 1777, British forces had taken over large areas of Canada and New York State. The patriots needed to keep the roads open for trade and to protect their supplies in New York and New England. On April 26, 1777, two thousand British troops invaded Connecticut by sea. They set fire to rebel ammunition and to houses in Danbury, Connecticut, only twelve miles away from Fredericksburgh, New York.

> *"Then guard your rights, Americans,*
> *Nor stoop to lawless sway,*
> *Oppose, oppose, oppose,*
> *For North America."*

Sixteen-year-old Sybil Ludington led her seven younger brothers and sisters in singing. Well, their singing was more like shouting. But Sybil knew that tonight Mama wouldn't care how noisy

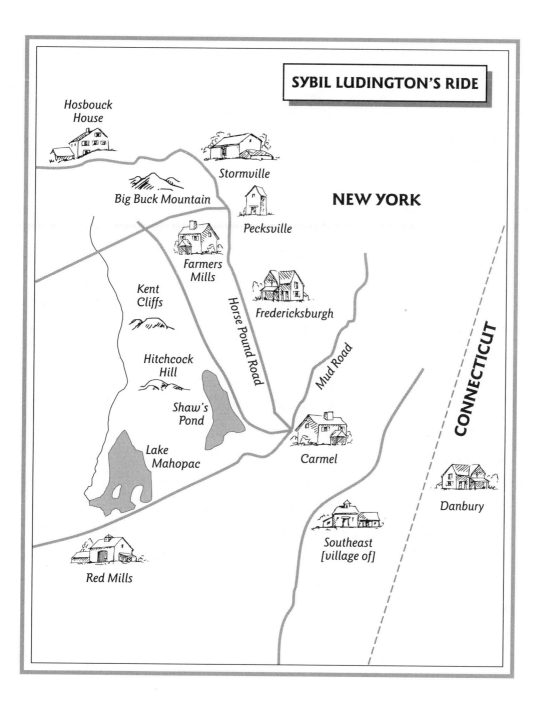

SYBIL LUDINGTON'S RIDE

Hosbouck
House

Stormville

Big Buck Mountain

NEW YORK

Pecksville

Farmers
Mills

Kent
Cliffs

Fredericksburgh

Horse Pound Road

Mud Road

Hitchcock
Hill

CONNECTICUT

Shaw's
Pond

Lake
Mahopac

Carmel

Danbury

Southeast
[village of]

Red Mills

they were. Papa was home on leave from the war. All the soldiers had been given two days' leave to help with spring planting. Even with the war on, life seemed good this April 26, 1777.

Mama lit the candles and the long oak table glowed, a warm contrast to the pounding April rain outside. At the brick oven, Sybil gave a last stir to the red kidney beans seasoned with salt pork and honey. Becky piled steaming corn bread on an earthenware platter. In front of Papa, Mary set a bowl of stew made thick with potatoes, carrots, cabbage, and turnips from the root cellar. Archie plopped a pitcher of maple syrup next to the fried parsnips.

Sybil squeezed in between Papa and her brother Archibald. Even though she didn't really feel like eating, she scooped up some stew and drenched her parsnips with syrup. She wanted to be outside, riding with Papa. But the vicious rain made that impossible tonight. Maybe tomorrow. As the oldest child in the family, Sybil was the only one allowed to ride with Papa. She loved racing with him to the parade grounds on their farm or trotting up and down the hills that made up his territory as commander of the Seventh Dutchess Militia. Sometimes when they galloped through the forest, Papa yelled "Tarnation," and she swore with him. Mama didn't like her to curse, but Sybil loved the sound of the word.

How she wished she could be a soldier and march off to fight the British, armed with her knife and gun! She touched the knife with the staghorn handle that Papa had given her four years ago. She wore it around her waist all the time. She also carried a twenty-eight-caliber pistol hidden under her shirt. Sybil was the family's protector when Papa was away. She could ride and shoot better than most boys her age. She had proven this over and over at contests. How unfair that girls were forbidden to join the militia, Sybil thought.

She knew the terrain of southern Dutchess County better than most men. From an early age, she had tracked down deer in the woods with her friend Nodjia. They scoured the rocky crevices and landings for signs as they watched for mountain lions and poisonous snakes. Nodjia was a Wappinger Indian and Sybil's best friend for as long as she could remember. Nodjia's people lived in the hills behind the Ludington farm. Sybil liked to dress like Nodjia in britches made of animal skins and moccasins. Of course, Nodjia didn't wear flannel shirts like Sybil, but she did carry a knife at her waist.

Bang! Bang! A sudden loud knocking hushed the family's boisterousness. Henry Ludington sprang to his feet. Sybil was at his heels as he opened the door.

A man with red, tired eyes and mud-soaked clothing saluted Sybil's father. The man's voice was urgent, but weak. "The British are burning Danbury. They torched the ammunition warehouses and set fire to barrels of pork and flour that were stored in the church. Now they're burning people's homes." He collapsed over the saddle. Sybil's father helped him down.

Tarnation! thought Sybil. Danbury, Connecticut, was only

twelve miles east, just across the border from her hometown. What if the British advanced on Fredericksburgh and burned the ammunition depot and homes here? They had controlled the city of New York since last August. Now they were trying to control the Hudson River highlands.

Someone had to muster her father's soldiers to stop the British. But Papa's soldiers were on leave. At this very minute they were probably eating with their families, too. It was clear the messenger was too weak to ride any farther. Papa had to stay here and wait for his troops to gather.

Without any hesitation, Sybil volunteered to round up the militia.

"No," her mother answered.

The creases between her father's eyebrows grew deeper. He spoke not a word. Sybil knew he was deciding whether or not to let her go. She stood by impatiently, hoping he would.

"It's a good forty miles round trip," he answered. His voice was as dry as the wood crackling in the fireplace.

Tarnation! She could race her chestnut colt, Star, for forty miles in the rain and dark. "I can do it, Papa. And I'll be careful, Mama."

Reluctantly, her parents gave their permission.

With not a moment to waste, she grabbed her father's cape from a hook in the pantry and ran out to the barn. She recited her orders to herself like a soldier. "Tell the troops to muster at Ludington's. We must stop the British from taking any more towns."

She tore open the barn doors. Star's ears straightened. His chestnut head with the white star shape shot high over the door of his stall. Sybil threw the hemp rope halter over Star's muzzle. Up went the weathered saddle onto his back. Off went her moccasins. Left foot first for good luck, she put on her boots, then hoisted herself into the saddle. How lucky that she always wore britches. Most women wore long skirts and had to ride sidesaddle. How ridiculous. Sybil always rode English-style, like a soldier.

It was about nine o'clock when she steered Star out of the barn and across the muddy, unplanted fields of her family's farm. Star snorted in the cold, damp air. His hooves sloshed through the soggy grass as they rode past the parade grounds and the family mill before they met the wet dirt of Mud Road. Sybil guided him along the thickly wooded path.

Shadows lurked everywhere. She fingered the knife at her waist. Her breath quickened as she scanned the thicket. At night loyalists roamed the countryside, stealing horses and cattle to sell to the British. They thought little about killing anyone who got in their way. Loyalist spies also hid in the woods. If they captured her and found out who she was, they might use her to lure her father into a trap. The British had offered a three-hundred-guinea reward for him.

No time to worry now. She had to ride the six miles to the village of Carmel as fast as she could.

"C'mon, boy." She urged Star forward. Sybil kept his gait to a trot. Too much galloping would strain his young legs. She broke a low-lying branch from a hickory tree to use when she got to the village.

Half an hour later, she rapped with the hickory on the windows of the first familiar house in Carmel. She knew every militiaman in her father's territory. "The British are burning Danbury," she shouted. When the sleepy occupants opened their shutters and looked out, she pointed to the fire and smoke in the east. "Spread the word to meet at the parade grounds at Ludington's." Her yell was fierce against the howling wind.

Tap! Tap! Her hickory woke the people at the next house. And the next. The village bell sounded the alarm. A man in a nightshirt ran out of his darkened house. "I'll ride with you," he offered.

"No," she hollered. "Go to the village of Southeast and pass the news on."

Sybil and Star dashed eastward through the murky night. The smell of drenched earth stung her nose. Suddenly the rain was more ferocious. She couldn't see more than a few inches ahead. The only light in the sky was from the enemy's fire. She tried to remember how the path looked in the brightness of day.

She squinted, and four lonely houses emerged from the dark alongside Shaw's Pond. "See the red sky!" she yelled. "The British are burning Danbury!" Her hoarse cry set dogs wailing. "The Seventh Dutchess must muster at Ludington's." Candles flickered in the dark houses as men raced to dress.

She rode through three lonely miles of thick fog to Lake Mahopac. The hilly path to the lake was slick and muddy. "Show me how surefooted you are, Star." She leaned over and patted him on his neck. He stumbled. She patted him again. "Come on, boy." With his every move, mud splattered up on her britches.

Now which way to go? Left? Right! Instinct told her to take the right fork to the mining town of Red Mills. She turned. There were deep, gravelly holes on this road. This would be a hard six miles. "Slow down, boy, slow down." She pulled on the reins until Star slowed to a walk.

Tarnation! Moving so cautiously meant that much longer to Red Mills. But under these conditions, she had no choice.

Two hours later, she rode into Red Mills, the halfway point in her journey. "Wake up!" she shouted. She rapped on the windows of the miners' cabins and yelled the urgent news. Candles flickered. The miners in her father's militia heard her!

No time to feel satisfied. She still had twenty miles to go. She hurried Star by the house abandoned by Colonel Roger Morris. Morris was a Tory. He had escaped to New York City, which the British controlled.

Now up Hitchcock Hill to the top. Star's legs fought hard against the slick rock. Papa's cape was soaked through. Sybil's wet shirt clung to her aching shoulders. She stretched out her arms and yanked at saplings along the way, hoping to keep herself and Star from falling. The wind ripped through the forest. Broken branches flew at them like daggers. Stones tore at her britches and boots. Star shook his head to keep the rain from blinding him. Sybil grasped the soaked hickory more tightly. "We can do this," she reassured him and herself.

Star found his footing again as he climbed to Kent Cliffs through the soggy pine forest. There were loyalists camped around here. One good thing about this blasted rain was that it would keep them tucked in their tents instead of roaming about.

I am a soldier, Sybil reminded herself. The thought quieted her fear.

At the bottom of the hill, where the valley began, the rain stopped. She took a breath. She heard water lapping from the lake, but she couldn't see the lake in the dark. "C'mon, boy." Star struggled to stay upright against the pull of the mud. "You can make it. Over the top to Farmers Mills," she said.

The road got so muddy that Star began to slip. He slowed down and secured his footing. It felt as if he was creeping up the hill. But, yes, there it was! She saw the post office. Farmers Mills! "The British are burning Danbury," she yelled. "Hurry to Ludington's!" Her cry was wild in the starless night. Tears filled her eyes as men ran out of their houses, muskets in their hands.

Mrs. Hasbrouck rushed out of her inn, a lantern in one hand, a mug of warm cider in the other. Sybil's mouth was so dry. She still had to cross the valley to Stormville. She slowed to take a gulp. Mrs. Hasbrouck's lantern guided her and Star out of the village. His

breathing was so heavy. Would he be able to go the distance?

There was a light drizzle now. The village clock sounded, and Star jerked. "Almost through, boy."

Up Big Buck Mountain. Ahead in the dark she made out the forms of men. She put her hand on her pistol. Were they friends or foes?

Suddenly a man passed her on horseback and yelled, "We heard the news, and we're on our way!" Her breathing quickened as she saw people scurrying about with lanterns.

Up Old Stormville Road.

Her message was getting through. Someone beat a hammer against the big iron ring on the village green, calling the soldiers to arms. Despite her tired, aching body, she felt happy.

"Oppose, oppose, oppose, for North America," she sang over and over to keep awake.

Five miles down Horse Pound Road to Pecksville, and another five to the parade grounds. Pecksville was the most familiar of all the towns. She always took the Mud Road shortcut to the log cabin schoolhouse. Sundays in good weather always found her at the Mountain Chapel, listening to Reverend White speak about the Lord.

"Muster at Ludington's," she shouted as she rode into town. A crowd of men was already gathered in the square, ready to leave.

"We're going home, Star," she said wearily.

On the last couple of miles, she could see the darkness lifting.

Soon it would be dawn. She passed men on horseback. They called to her in greeting. She made out the familiar faces of some of her father's soldiers. They were farmers and fishermen and miners. All were patriots determined to fight to the death for independence.

On the parade grounds, she saw Papa and hundreds of men, already drilling. Tarnation! She was successful. She saluted her father. Some soldiers called out their thanks. Without her, they wouldn't be here. She had ridden harder and had covered more territory than any soldier in Papa's militia tonight.

Because Sybil Ludington mustered the men in her father's regiment on the evening of April 26, 1777, the Seventh Dutchess Militia from New York joined the Continental troops and Connecticut militia forces just outside Danbury, Connecticut, for the Battle of Ridgefield the next day. The patriots forced the British to flee to their ships in Compo (now Westport), Connecticut. Most historical accounts of the battle do not mention the role of Henry Ludington's regiment; our research uncovered a biography of Henry Ludington, written in 1907, which mentioned a letter of gratitude from Colonel Alexander Hamilton to Gouverneur Morris of New York. Hamilton wrote, "I congratulate you on the Danbury expedition. The spirit of the people on the occasion does them great honor. . . . "

Sybil never got her wish to enlist in the army, but she was honored as a patriot. General George Washington and the French Comte de Rochambeau visited her home to thank her. After the war ended, she was soon forgotten.

Today her achievement is being recognized. Her birthplace,

Fredericksburgh, New York, has renamed itself Ludingtonville. Roadside markers now trace her route. In 1974 the United States Postal Service honored her with an eight-cent stamp. A sculpture of Sybil and Star, by Anna Hyatt Huntington, stands on the shore of Shaw's Pond, which is now called Lake Gleneida. Another stands outside the public library in Danbury, Connecticut. Huntington chose to sculpt Sybil in a colonial-era dress. Though romanticized, the statues are a tribute to Sybil's achievement.

A QUESTION OF JUSTICE:
Grace Growden Galloway

✦

On September 11, 1777, the British forced the Americans to retreat at Brandywine Crossing, Pennsylvania. Two weeks later, on September 26, General Howe triumphantly led his troops into Philadelphia. Philadelphia's loyalists welcomed them.

The British remained for nine months. On June 15, 1778, Howe ordered his ten thousand men to evacuate the city. More than three thousand loyalists left with them. Grace Growden Galloway was married to a loyalist. Her husband fled, but she stayed in Philadelphia to secure her inheritance. Like other loyalists, she found her once-privileged life and property threatened. In the eyes of the patriots, she was a traitor.

Grace Growden Galloway tried to concentrate on what her friend Molly Craig was saying, but it was impossible. All the windows in her home were locked, and she was stifling hot on this humid August afternoon in 1778. Her ring finger distractedly tapped the edge of the china cup on the tea table in the parlor. She breathed in the temporary comfort of familiar objects. She loved her handsome home in Philadelphia. But soon her mahogany writing desk and every other treasured object would be taken away and sold. All because of Joseph.

Three furious knocks at the front door interrupted Molly's chatter. Grace didn't even look up. She knew who was banging and had no intention of responding. A servant ran into the parlor and asked her what to do. Molly looked toward Grace, waiting for her answer. Grace sat erect in her chair and calmly repeated her lawyer's instructions: Shut all the doors and windows. Don't let them in, except by force.

Two months ago, when the British sailed from Philadelphia to New York, Grace's husband, Joseph, and their twenty-year-old daughter, Elizabeth, went with them. Joseph was a prominent loyalist and feared Philadelphia's patriots would take revenge on him if he stayed. Grace feared for her daughter's safety and insisted that Elizabeth leave with him. Joseph was right to be afraid. Many loyalists had been arrested. One was hanged, and there were rumors of more hangings.

The pounding got louder. It was hard not to feel angry with Joseph. His arrogance had put her in this fragile situation. Joseph was forever sure that his opinions were correct. He was a delegate at the First Continental Congress and one of the most powerful men in Pennsylvania. He served eighteen years in the Pennsylvania Assembly, eight as speaker. From the very beginning, he proclaimed with absolute certainty that most Americans would not support the revolution. His wealth blinded him to the determination of the rebels. His dear friend Benjamin Franklin had tried to convince him to support independence. But Joseph refused.

If only he had kept silent. Not Joseph. He never kept silent. During the uproar over the Stamp Act, he wrote articles stating that Parliament had the right to tax Americans. He used a pseudonym, but Philadelphia's patriots quickly deduced that he was "Americanus." In December 1776 he crossed the line and joined the British army. He gathered intelligence from his network of loyalist spies. Grace couldn't deny that Joseph was effective. In one raid his volunteer militia of loyalists seized all the cloth in Bucks County that women were spinning for the Continental army. Eight Americans were killed during the raid. Giving ammunition or supplies or information to the British was treason. Treason was punishable by death and loss of property.

When the English army marched into Philadelphia last year, General Howe had rewarded Joseph for his loyalty. He was appointed superintendent general of police and superintendent of the port. Joseph issued rules that made Philadelphians feel like prisoners in their own city. No wonder he was so despised.

Now the patriots were pounding at her door. They had come to remove her from her home. Joseph was out of reach, but his property was not. They would sell the house or rent it as they pleased. They would take all his property, including Grace's land inherited from her father. That land was worth more than thirteen thousand pounds sterling. Trevose, her estate in Bucks County just northeast of Philadelphia, was one of the grandest in the county.

Under the law, a woman's property—land, money, and jewelry—all went to her husband during their lives together, unless the couple agreed before marriage to do otherwise. Grace and Joseph had not signed such an agreement, so her land belonged to him. And since it was his land, the patriots believed they had the right to seize it.

She *couldn't* let them take her land. She needed it for her daughter. Elizabeth required a substantial dowry to marry a man of quality.

The banging intensified. She couldn't ignore it any longer. She walked out of the parlor to the front door. "I am in possession of my own house and will keep it so. You will not gain admission," she called out. The banging stopped immediately, but Grace knew the men outside would not give up.

Within minutes three men burst into the kitchen. Grace thrust her lawyer's letter at Charles Willson Peale, a well-known artist and fervent patriot. Peale read it hurriedly, then passed it on. The letter stated her legal right to stay in the house. One by one, the men dismissed the letter with equal contempt.

"I have studied the law, too," Peale said with a sneer, "and what we did was right."

"You shall never get me out from this house, except by force,"

Grace answered.

"Oh, you'll leave," he said confidently, "when we throw your clothes into the street. We've moved more than forty women out of their houses."

"But they were all allowed to take their furniture with them," she responded.

"Their husbands did not treat people as cruelly as yours did."

Grace did not respond.

Peale switched tactics. "I have a carriage waiting to take you wherever you want to go," he said.

Grace's head pounded. Her palms were sweaty. She resisted the impulse to argue. She knew that there was no way to win this confrontation. She had to leave, at least temporarily. She nodded her consent.

"We'll need our hats. And the bag on the chair upstairs," Grace answered.

"I'll get it." Peale disappeared upstairs and returned with a small bag and two bonnets.

"Allow her at least to take her bed," said Molly.

"She can take nothing else," Peale said. He thrust one bonnet into Grace's hand and the other into Molly's. Then his voice softened. "Come, Mrs. Galloway. Give me your hand."

"Indeed I will not." Grace turned and looked at Molly. "Pray, take notice," she announced. "I do not leave of my own accord, but by force."

Peale grabbed her arm.

"Mr. Peale, let go of my arm. You are the last man on earth I wish to be obliged to." She threw back her shoulders and walked slowly down the stairs.

Molly stepped up into the carriage and offered her hand to Grace. Grace carefully gathered the skirt of her only gown and accepted her friend's hand. Molly gave the driver her address, and the carriage pulled away.

Grace's stomach tightened. She was homeless, with no means of support. Molly was taking her in, but she couldn't stay with her friend forever. Her lawyer had said that she could sue for damages against forcible entry, but that was of little consolation now.

Months passed. Grace stayed with Molly and her family. Her carriage and all the furniture were sold at auction. She received no money from the sale. Everything was gone. Elizabeth's books and baby tea chest had been auctioned off. Oh, how she had wanted to buy her daughter's possessions, but she could not raise the fifteen pounds sterling to do so.

Another friend, Deborah Morris, invited Grace to stay with her family. Grace accepted the invitation, but her friend's kindness could not stop her growing feeling of isolation. She had had such a large circle of friends, but hardly anyone visited her now. They were afraid the patriots would retaliate if they befriended Joseph Galloway's wife. Even her lawyer was cold to her.

Joseph wrote her from New York, urging her to join him and Elizabeth. She refused. She had to get back her property so Elizabeth would not become a beggar, too.

In late October a friend smuggled in a letter from Joseph saying that he and Elizabeth were sailing for England. At least Elizabeth was safe and away from danger. But Elizabeth's absence made Grace feel even lonelier, for now there was no one in the colonies who loved her. She spent most days in bed. Her feet swelled. She knew she should get up and go outside and walk, but she could not bring herself to do so.

In December Grace learned that Joseph had received four hundred pounds sterling in rent from *her* inherited estates. She was enraged. Here she was without a farthing, and he hadn't shared anything with her. If it weren't for Elizabeth, she would have nothing to do with him ever again. Their marriage had always been turbulent. Even in his absence, he caused her unrest.

Over the next two years, all of Grace's inherited land was sold. Joseph received money from each sale but sent her none. Despite the continued goodness of a few friends, she felt more and more hopeless. Her spirits and health worsened. The doctor prescribed many different medicines, but none helped. She thought about going to London to be with Elizabeth, but she felt too weak to undertake the three-to-six-week sea journey. Her health deteriorated until she was too sick to leave her bed. In the fall of 1781, she gathered her strength and wrote her daughter:

Dearest Elizabeth,

I am still in Philadelphia. I sit in my room as ignorant of all the grand bustle of life as any recluse or pious person in this or former ages. When I am free from pain, I quilt and read. I care little for the world, but want to be esteemed by all good people I love.

It is now going on three years since I was left in this dreadful situation. My health is now so impaired that I never hope to have it in my power to see my relations or native country again. My health and the desire to save your inheritance alone detain me. If I save my child, all will be right. I am not like the same person in any thing but my unbounded affection for you and my concern for your welfare.

Affectionately yours,
Mother

Grace Galloway died shortly before sunset on February 6, 1782. She was fifty-five years old. She willed her confiscated estate to her daughter, even though under law it still belonged to her husband.

Elizabeth did not forget the lesson of her mother's tragic death. When she married, she insisted that her husband sign a contract giving her and her children sole ownership of her inheritance from her father. Joseph Galloway died in 1803. He willed his wife's estate to his daughter.

Elizabeth's lawyers took legal action to ensure that she received it. In 1804 the case reached the Pennsylvania Supreme Court. The judges decided that Grace's property rightfully belonged to her heirs. After twenty-six years, the wrongs against Grace Growden Galloway were finally righted.

THE SPY:

James Armistead

In June 1778 France entered the war on the side of the Americans. Military action turned to the southern colonies—to Savannah, Georgia; to Charleston and the South Carolina countryside; to North Carolina; and, finally, to Virginia. By spring 1781 the Marquis de Lafayette, a twenty-three-year-old French nobleman, commanded the small American army in Virginia. His opponents were commanders Benedict Arnold and Charles Cornwallis.

James Armistead crouched in the brush on the hill near his owner's plantation in New Kent, Virginia. He took out a spool of wire from his pouch. If he was lucky, he and the other slaves on the plantation would feast tonight on the crisp skin and rich meat of a roasted hog. It was mid-March 1781. James was hungry. He had been hungry for four years, ever since the British began their vicious campaign of destroying life in Virginia. They had burned anything and everything—tobacco, pork, rum, salt, oats, wheat,

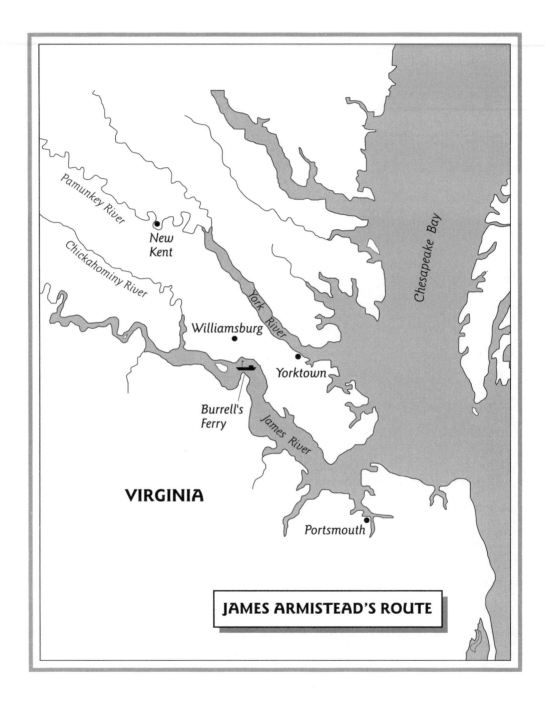

Pamunkey River

New
Kent

Chickahominy River

York River

Williamsburg

Yorktown

Burrell's
Ferry

James River

Chesapeake Bay

VIRGINIA

Portsmouth

JAMES ARMISTEAD'S ROUTE

and, of course, gunpowder.

James made a hoop and tied a slip noose to serve as the snare for the hog. From his pouch he took squirrel meat wrapped in a mullein leaf. He carefully put it through the snare on the far side so the hog would have to go through the hoop to get it. No hog could resist raw meat. He held the long end of his wire and placed the hoop on the path at the height of a hog's head. Now all he had to do was wait.

He climbed up a catalpa tree, fresh in bloom. The tree's common name was elephant ears because of its large leaves. He loved the sweet fragrance of its white flower petals and the purple lines running through them. From his perch in a low branch, he looked across the ridge and saw patches of burnt earth and buildings. To the south he saw the sails of British warships and smaller frigates in the James River. James Armistead feared the British merchant sailors. They kidnapped slaves and shipped them to the West Indies to be sold.

Suddenly he heard a succession of grunts from behind the thick shrubs and vines. A fat one, he hoped. He shimmied down the tree and gripped the wire of the snare as tautly as possible. Leaves and twigs rustled as the pig tore through the woods toward him.

When the black hog reached the snare, it smelled the meat and snorted in delight. It poked its head through the wire and sniffed more closely. Now! James pulled the slip noose tight. Ah, victory! The pig was trapped.

William Armistead's plantation was just over the rise, but James had to kill the hog, then gut it here. Otherwise, gas from its stomach would build up, and his treasure would go bad. Carefully and steadily, he cut a slit down the hog's muscular middle. He reached in and pulled out its stomach and digestive organs. He wrapped the tasty innards in large, bristly mullein leaves as a present for his owner. He wiped his hands clean with other mullein leaves. Dragging his treasure behind him, he started back to the plantation.

He hung the hog by its hind feet from a log tacked across the top of his cabin. After a quick stop by the kitchen of the Big House, he went to see his owner. William Armistead was in the barn, staring at a couple hundred bushels of last fall's wheat he had managed to scrounge from neighboring plantations. A few weeks ago, Armistead had been appointed commissary by the Virginia Assembly. His job was to supply food, blankets, and guns to the troops of "the marquis." That's what every patriot affectionately called Major General Lafayette.

Lafayette's formal name was Marie-Joseph-Paul-Yves-Roch-Gilbert du Motier, Marquis de Lafayette. He had sailed to America with other wealthy Europeans who supported the colonial uprising. He won George Washington's respect and was now a major general in the Continental army.

"Did you catch a hog?" William Armistead asked.

"A fat one," James answered. "I gave the cook the innards."

William Armistead nodded. James knew without his owner saying it that he appreciated the gift.

For the rest of the afternoon, James loaded wheat and boxes of ammunition into a wagon. Tomorrow at sunrise, he would leave the plantation. Lafayette had asked his owner to find intelligent Negro men who knew the Virginia terrain to serve as spies. William Armistead had volunteered James. He was to go to the marquis's headquarters at Williamsburg tomorrow morning.

That evening James shared the hog with the other slaves on the plantation. The feast was a welcome break from their everyday toil.

Just before sunrise, he tucked his long white shirt into his breeches, put on his straw hat, and hurried to the barn. His slave pass was safe in his pouch along with his knife and a spool of wire. Instinctively he patted the pouch and was relieved to hear the crinkle of paper. He never went anywhere without the slave pass.

The farm overseer patted the horse's rump, and they began the fifteen-mile journey to Williamsburg. The sun shone golden. The smell of the fresh spring mud in the chilly morning air pleased James. It had rained hard the past few weeks, and James knew it would be a wet and soggy ride down the peninsula between the York and Chickahominy Rivers. But on such a beautiful morning he didn't mind. He cushioned himself against the bushel bags of wheat as the wagon bounced along the ravine.

Big farms lay on both sides of the ravine. The tallest thing in sight was the tower of St. Peter's Church.

The wagon's wheels fought the swampy ground beneath them

on the narrow road. A number of creeks and streams drained into the Chickahominy and the York. Diascund Creek was the biggest and muddiest. James took a deep breath as they approached it. Predictably, one of the wagon wheels got stuck.

He rolled up his pants and jumped down from the wagon into the creek so the overseer would not become angry. James's winter shoes were going to get very muddy and irritate his feet while they dried, but he had no choice. He tensed his leg muscles and secured his feet in the thick mud.

"Push," the overseer ordered. James put his strong hands on the wagon wheel and did as he was told.

"Pull," the overseer shouted at the horse, whipping him. James flinched, even though the whip was not meant for him. The combined strength of James and the horse budged the wagon.

After ten miles they reached Hickory Neck Church near Burnt Ordinary. Everyone called the one-time wooden tavern by that name since the British had burned it down. The road flattened. It was noon when they entered Williamsburg.

The overseer headed for the magazine, where the Continental army stored its gunpowder. He went off to eat with the soldiers and left James to unpack the supplies.

When he returned for James, he drove the wagon directly to the marquis's headquarters. Two rows of catalpa trees about one hundred paces apart lined the green leading into Palace Street and a row of stately houses. The wagon stopped at a two-story, brick residence with two chimneys. Tiny crocus shoots poked through the grass. A sole buckeye tree in bloom emitted a sweet smell. James felt nervous walking up the path. What would the marquis be like?

A tall, dark-skinned man answered the overseer's knock. He asked James to wait outside and led the overseer into the parlor. Through the partially opened parlor door, James heard the overseer greet Lafayette.

The man led James around the back of the house to the kitchen. Several colored women were cooking. One of them gave him a slice of bread.

The overseer was gone when the man brought him back to the parlor. The marquis was seated at a table piled high with maps. James tried not to stare but quickly decided that the marquis was about his age. He had hazel eyes and a light complexion. His wig was white, but James could tell from his eyebrows that his hair was sandy-colored. He wore a white ruffled shirt, black tie, and gold-brocaded vest. A dark blue sash lay across his chest. His jacket was dark blue with gold buttons and trimmed in gold. Shiny black boots covered his white breeches up to his knees. He seemed shorter than James, but he was fancier than James had imagined.

"I understand you know these parts well," Lafayette said.

"Yes sir."

"Can you find your way to Portsmouth?"

"Yes sir."

Lafayette explained that James was to go to the headquarters of

Benedict Arnold, the British commander in Portsmouth. Arnold was an American who had been a major general in the Continental army. He had betrayed the patriots by spying for the British. Now Arnold was trying to blockade the Chesapeake Bay harbor, so the southern states could not ship their crops overseas. This would bankrupt the colonial economy. The Americans wouldn't have any money to buy supplies and ammunition from France.

"I have a Negro spy in service at Commander Arnold's table," Lafayette explained. James was to carry a letter in code for him. If he arrived safely, he would deliver the letter and bring back whatever information the spy had about Arnold's plans and the strength of his forces. James was impressed. He had heard of slaves who could read or write, but he didn't know any.

"Can you accomplish what I ask?" asked Lafayette.

"Yes sir."

"You'll know my man by his blue ink quill," said Lafayette. "Tell him you can supply the officers' table with fresh food, and he'll know I sent you."

James departed immediately. Outside he saw several buckeye nuts on the grass. He put them into his pouch and set out on the forty-mile trek to Portsmouth. The trip would take him ten hours, and he would arrive in the dark.

He went due south until he came to Burrell's Ferry. Even before he was asked, he showed his slave pass to the ferry captain. There was no way of knowing if the man was a loyalist or patriot. Lafayette had told him that if the ferry captain asked any questions, he should say that he was foraging for supplies for his owner.

Disembarking on the south side of the river, James kept close to the tall grasses. He needed cover to hide from slave patrols and merchant sailors. Nearly half of Virginia's population in the Tidewater region was of African descent. The British had promised freedom to any slave who joined their army. Virginia's white plantation owners were furious, for hundreds of his people had run away. James had heard rumors that so many slaves had joined the redcoats that every officer had at least three servants and two cooks. Like all slaves, he had thought about running away to the British army. But how could he be sure the British would really free him after the war was over? He also had heard that colored servants at British camps were treated like slaves. He preferred to forage for William Armistead in the open air than be a servant for the British.

The soil here was softer, drier, and sandier than on the north side of the river. James was glad, because his feet were tired and irritated. It was getting dark. He had to be cautious not to step on poisonous copperheads. There would be more vermin as he neared Portsmouth. No time to worry now. He took the buckeye nuts from his pouch. He had an important task: to bring a present for Benedict Arnold's table to begin to win his favor.

He rubbed his hands together, crushed the shells, and removed the seeds. He inhaled the strong, sweet aroma that escaped. Why did people call it the stinky tree? he wondered.

With seeds in his closed fist, he walked to the river's edge. Luckily, the air held a breeze and the sky was overcast. He hoped for trout but saw only catfish in the shallow river water. He waded in up to his knees. The fish were jumping six to eight inches into the air for flies. He opened his fist and tossed in the buckeye seeds. They floated for a few moments until the catfish ate them. Suddenly the fish stopped jumping. They lay on their sides and appeared dead. It had worked. The seeds had stunned them. With the long cloth of his shirt, James scooped up twenty catfish and waded out of the water. Back on shore, he cut some wire and tied them together by their tails. Then he killed and gutted them. Now he had his gift for Benedict Arnold.

When he arrived at the British camp, he saw hundreds of colored men, women, and children milling about. The former slaves wore an assortment of clothes—discarded coats and hats of British soldiers, parts of American uniforms, and silk breeches and waistcoats probably stolen from their owners. Barefoot women walked about in fancy robes. He had never seen so many of his people gathered in one place. It felt good. Had he made the right decision to remain a slave?

British soldiers were milling about with pale, sickly faces. Many could barely stand. The sickest ones were on stretchers being carried into the barracks. The British cannot adjust to the swamps and mosquitoes, he thought.

A soldier with a lantern approached. James's throat got dry. The marquis's letter was at the front of his mind. He had to deliver it safely. "State your name and purpose," commanded the soldier.

James quietly coughed the dryness out of his throat. "My name is James. I escaped." He held up the cluster of catfish for the soldier to see. "I brought fish for Commander Arnold," he answered.

"Trying to buy your freedom with fish? That's a new one," the soldier mocked.

Nonetheless, he led James to the kitchen in Benedict Arnold's headquarters. Two colored women were stirring food in large cauldrons over the fire. One woman took the fish. A cocoa-colored man in clean breeches and a white shirt with a collar was stacking dishes. His eyes met James's. Was he the spy? He pointed for James to sit at a wooden table and brought him a piece of freshly baked bread.

James chewed slowly and listened to voices coming from the other side of the kitchen door. Was one of them Benedict Arnold's?

The man in the white shirt stood before James. "Are you looking for work?" he asked.

"Yes," James answered. Was this Lafayette's spy? He didn't have a blue quill. But maybe he was the spy. He would try out the marquis's phrase and then he would know. "I can supply the officers' table with fresh food," he said. He thought he saw a slight smile on the man's face. But he wasn't sure.

"Did you catch the fish yourself?" the man asked.

James nodded.

"Wait in the barn," the man whispered. "I'll come after the commander finishes his dinner."

A row of well-groomed horses whinnied in their stalls. James knew they were most likely stolen from Virginia plantation owners like William Armistead. He sat down on a pile of hay to wait. He heard men's voices but couldn't distinguish what they were saying. Squinting through the cracks in the barn walls, he could see only forms in the dark. Were the men coming for him? Their voices grew close. The speech was slurred. Probably British soldiers who had drunk too much wine. Such men could be unpredictable and dangerous. The door swung open. James jumped to his feet.

"Shhh," someone whispered. In the lantern light, James was relieved to see the man in the white shirt. This time he had a blue jay quill in his pocket.

"Do you have something for me?" the man asked.

James gave him the coded letter.

"I'll come back when I can," the man said.

When he returned, he spoke softly. "Go back to the marquis. Tell him that Arnold and his men are trapped here in Portsmouth. Virginia militia surround them on all sides. We have little here, and many soldiers are sick. Only our people are strong enough to build trenches." A look of pride passed between them. "Hide here tonight and leave before sunrise. No one will see you." The man closed the barn door behind him.

James was up and gone well before sunrise. On the way back to

Williamsburg, he stopped briefly to eat fiddlehead ferns. He wrapped some extras in mullein leaves for the marquis.

Several weeks later, General Charles Cornwallis, British commander of the southern campaign, joined forces with Arnold. Together they raided Virginia up and down the York and James Rivers. They confiscated eight hundred horses from plantation owners and built a mighty cavalry. For the rest of the year, Lafayette and Cornwallis fought hit-and-run battles through the swamps and Tidewater area of Virginia. Lafayette continued to rely upon James for information. James went back and forth between Benedict Arnold's camp and Lafayette's headquarters. He won Arnold's respect as a forager and became a trusted worker. He used his eyes and ears to find out what Arnold was planning and reported this back to the marquis.

In May 1781 Lafayette sent him to spy on Cornwallis. James won favor with Cornwallis and his aides, as he had with Arnold, and again gathered information. Cornwallis never suspected that James was an American spy. In fact, he trusted him so much that he asked James to go to Williamsburg and insinuate himself into Lafayette's headquarters to spy on the marquis. Over the months, Lafayette gave James invented reports to pass on to Cornwallis. The British commander never suspected that James was really spying for the Americans.

On August 25, 1781, Lafayette wrote to Washington that he received the information about Cornwallis's camp in Yorktown from "a sensible fellow" who would "keep open a channel of the most useful communications."

This "sensible fellow" was James Armistead. The intelligence that James and other African-American spies obtained helped bring about the end of the war on October 19, 1781, at the Battle of Yorktown.

In November 1784 James and Lafayette met in Richmond, Virginia. The marquis gave James a letter certifying that he had delivered "services to me while I had the honour to command in this state. His intelligence from the enemy's camp were industriously collected and more faithfully delivered. He perfectly acquitted himself with some important commissions I gave him and appears to me entitled to every reward his situation can admit of" (as found in Quarles, The Negro in the American Revolution).

In autumn 1786 the General Assembly of Virginia freed James. He shed his slave name Armistead and took the surname Lafayette. In 1819 he finally received a pension from Virginia for his services as a spy.

James and Lafayette met again on October 27, 1824, when the marquis visited Richmond for the first time since the war. James was standing in the street with other Virginians who had come out to honor Lafayette. Riding in an open carriage, Lafayette saw Armistead and jumped down to greet him. The unusual event of an international hero embracing a Negro man was recorded in the newspapers of the time.

THE RECRUIT:
Robert Shurtliff

Peace talks between the English and Americans began after the Battle of Yorktown, but fighting in the central part of what is now New York State continued between American patriots and loyalists and their Indian allies. From the beginning, patriots and loyalists pursued the six tribes of the Iroquois Confederacy to become their allies. The Iroquois Confederacy stayed out of the conflict until July 1777, when British promises of future trade and land security convinced the Mohawk, Cayuga, Seneca, and Onondaga to go over to the British side. The Oneida and Tuscarora joined forces with the Americans.

After the Battle of Yorktown, Mohawk leader Joseph Brant formed a militia that included both Mohawk fighters and thirty-one loyalists. His militia began attacking settlements. In May 1782 Washington issued the call for recruits to squelch these attacks.

Robert Shurtliff reached his long, muscular arms across the table to pick up a pile of dirty plates. He was used to cleaning up other people's messes. He preferred working at Sproats Tavern in Middleborough, Massachusetts, to most other jobs. At least here, in between serving and cleaning, he could listen to the men talk about what it had been like to be in battle. But tonight's talk was not of past victories. Tonight the tavern buzzed with the news that George Washington was calling for new recruits to combat the roaming bands of loyalists attacking settlements in western New York.

Robert had followed every military action since the war began seven years ago. He had wanted to enlist right after Lexington and Concord. He was fifteen then. Boys as young as fourteen were going off to war, but he couldn't go. He was working off his time as an indentured servant to Jeremiah Thomas. He had watched regretfully as, one by one, all ten of Thomas's sons left to serve their country. Robert took over their work, toiling long hours in the fields, plowing and planting and mending fences. He was as strong and sturdy as any of the Thomas men.

Over the clatter of dishes, Robert heard the same comments again and again. Most men said they'd already sacrificed enough for the revolution. They had left their families and farms and businesses to fight. They had done their duty as patriots. It was time for them to take care of their families.

Robert didn't have family responsibilities. He didn't own a farm or business. No longer an indentured servant, he was free to do what he wanted. As he saw it, joining the army would mean the end of his dull life. It isn't too late to be a soldier, he thought, soaping the dishes.

Late that night he took scissors to his thick hair. He didn't have a looking glass to see how well he was cutting it, but he didn't let that stop him. Slowly and methodically, he cut his blond waves until layers of them covered the floor. Then he pulled his hair back over his ears and tied it into a bob, as was the style for men. He ran his hand over his beardless face. Hopefully his new companions would not comment on it. But if they did, he was determined not to let this bother him. The only thing that was important now was realizing his long-cherished dream of becoming a soldier.

He donned a new ruffled white shirt, a coarse brown cotton coat, and tan breeches. The clothes fit nicely over his lean, muscular body. He pulled up his sturdy farm boots. They were ill-suited for his new outfit but would serve him well on long marches. All in all, at five feet, eight inches, he knew he cut a handsome figure.

Relatives said he resembled the Shurtliff side. He hardly remembered his father, who had abandoned the family shortly after his seventh child was conceived.

He buttoned his coat and took one last look around him, then stepped out into the cold night.

Early morning on Monday, May 20, 1782, Robert completed his twenty-five-mile walk to Bellingham. He went straight to the town tavern and told Noah Taft, the mustering officer, that he had come to serve his country. He signed his name in the record book.

Taft examined his bold signature and pronounced him a soldier in the Massachusetts Fourth Regiment in the Continental army. He paid Robert sixty pounds sterling, deducting a small fee for signing him up.

Robert Shurtliff looked into the mirror of his small dressing room in Boston's Federal Street Theatre. It was March 22, 1802, almost twenty years since he had served in the Massachusetts Fourth Regiment. He still cut a handsome figure in his blue and white uniform, even though he was somewhat thicker around the waist than he had been then.

Dressing tonight was easier than it had been when he was an enlisted man. He didn't have to wait to dress until the rest of the regiment left the barracks. He didn't have to wrap his chest with that uncomfortable cloth as he had then. And he no longer worried about his beardless face.

After military service Robert had returned to Stoughton, Massachusetts, to work on his uncle's farm. He had put away his uniform, never thinking he would wear it again. His life now, at age forty-two, was conventional. Giving lectures about being a soldier had been a good idea. He hadn't been sure that anyone would come to hear him. Some people called the very idea of his speaking on a public stage "shocking" and "scandalous" and refused to come.

A newspaper reporter named Herman Mann had assured Robert that people would come to hear him. Robert didn't completely trust Herman Mann. He had spent long hours telling Mann about his war experiences. Mann had shaped the interviews into a book. When Robert read the memoir, he was angry and disappointed. It was filled with exaggerations and half-truths. He had told Mann in no uncertain terms to correct the errors in the next printing.

But Mann had been right about people coming tonight. There were three hundred people in the theater. He would make a nice profit this evening. He needed the money. Bringing up four children as a farmer had not proven profitable. Besides, why shouldn't he get the same recognition and respect that other soldiers had gotten?

He was still owed money for his military service. Last year he petitioned the Massachusetts Senate for it. Paul Revere wrote a letter in his support; the senate had not yet ruled on his petition.

There was a gentle knock on the door. Time to go. He took a last look in the mirror and walked toward the wings. When the announcer said his name, he shouldered his musket, marched to the front of the stage, and stood at attention. Let the audience see how tall and erect a soldier can be. Let the audience see his immaculately pressed blue and white uniform and his shiny boots.

Now to dazzle them! Let them see proof that Robert Shurtliff was as competent a soldier as any man could be. He bit off the end of the cartridge paper and stuffed powder into the musket's pan. He stood the musket on its fat end and dropped the remaining

powder, ball, and rolled-up paper into the barrel. He pushed it all down with a ramrod. Then he raised his musket, held it level with the ground, and pretended to pull back the flints, as if ready to fire. He flinched in preparation of the musket fire he had heard so many times. Then he relaxed. This was only for show.

He cleared his voice and smiled. "I know what you are thinking," he said in a deep, rich voice. He heard a few gasps. His voice was one reason that he had fooled everyone in the regiment. No one had realized then who he was. No one. Not Noah Taft. Not his commander. Not any of the soldiers in the Massachusetts Fourth Regiment. No one had realized he was a woman whose real name was Deborah Samson.

"You are thinking," Deborah continued, "what made this woman slope from the soft sphere of her own sex to face the storms both of elements and the war?"

She paused, as if waiting for an answer to the question. "For several years I looked upon the war without being able to join. I looked upon the scenes of havoc and devastation at Lexington and Concord and Bunker Hill without being able to extend a rescuing hand. Then with an enthusiasm and frenzy that could brook not control, I burst the tyrant bonds, which custom and the world denied women, and became a warrior. I secretly grasped an opportunity, which the world seemed to deny, as a natural privilege. I prepared for battle."

She stopped again. She knew her audience was expecting her to apologize for being "unladylike" by disguising herself as a man and becoming a soldier. Mr. Mann had insisted she apologize. She didn't feel she had done anything wrong. She continued, "I am indeed willing to acknowledge what I have done. Perhaps an error, because I swerved from the accustomed flowery path of female delicacy. I left my morning pillow of roses to a couch of brambles for the night. But I did it."

Deborah Samson inhaled deeply. She was proud to have been a soldier. She was glad to finally tell her story.

This was the first of six lectures given by Deborah Samson in Massachusetts and New York. We do not have the text of any other lecture, but we assume she probably gave the same talk again and again. Herman Mann wrote this first lecture.

Samson got Mann to make some corrections in the memoir, but he never corrected his misspelling of her name—Sampson. This incorrect spelling went down in the history books, and many people, even historians, still use it.

Even today historians have trouble separating fact from fiction about Samson's life. Here's what we know is true about her: She served for seven months with the Massachusetts Fourth Regiment, but the extent of her participation in skirmishes against Joseph Brant's militia remains un-documented.

She married a farmer named Benjamin Gannet on April 7, 1785. She finally got her pension and back pay in January 1803. She died on

April 27, 1827. She is buried in Rock Ridge Cemetery, near Sharon, Massachusetts.

Even though we do not yet know all the details of Samson's military life, her courage to defy the myth that women are unsuited for combat and to risk her life on the battlefield has earned her an important place in history. In 1983 her home state, Massachusetts, recognized her courage: Governor Michael J. Dukakis declared Deborah Samson the Official Heroine of the Commonwealth and set aside May 23 in acknowledgment of the anniversary of her enlistment. In 1985 the U.S. Capitol Historical Society in Washington, D.C., issued a commemorative medal in her honor. Fortunately Samson was spelled correctly both times.

Deborah Samson's desire to fight for her country and her disguise as a man to do so were unconventional, daring acts for a woman of her time. The fact that historians cannot yet verify many things about her life does not diminish her commitment to her country or her military service.

IMPORTANT EVENTS

1765 The Stamp Act requires colonists to pay taxes on printed matter; they refuse.

1766 Parliament repeals the Stamp Act.

1767 The Townshend Acts tax tea and other goods.

March 5, 1770 The Boston Massacre, a confrontation between British troops and angry Bostonians, erupts into shooting; three Americans are killed.

1773 Francis Salvador arrives in Charlestown (Charleston), South Carolina, from London.

December 16, 1773 Patriots disguised as Indians throw chests of tea into Boston Harbor to protest the tax on tea.

September 5–October 26, 1774 All colonies send delegates to the First Continental Congress in Philadelphia to protest the Intolerable Acts.

January 10, 1775 Thomas Paine's *Common Sense* is published anonymously.

April 19, 1775 Paul Revere, Bill Dawes, and Dr. Samuel Prescott ride to warn the colonists that the British are marching to Concord. Lexington and Concord mark the first battles of the American Revolution. Peter Salem from Framingham, Massachusetts, fights at Lexington.

May 10, 1775 American General Benedict Arnold and the Green Mountain Boys, led by Ethan Allen, capture Fort

Ticonderoga on Lake Champlain in New York.

June 7, 1775 The colonies decide to call themselves the United States.

June 15, 1775 The Second Continental Congress appoints George Washington as commander in chief of the Continental army.

June 17, 1775 Peter Brown and Peter Salem fight in the Battle of Bunker Hill.

August 31, 1775 Francis Salvador gets signatures for the loyalty oath.

March 2, 1776 The Americans begin the bombardment of Boston.

March 17, 1776 General Sir William Howe and seven thousand British soldiers leave Boston in defeat.

March 31, 1776 Abigail Adams writes John Adams to "Remember the Ladies."

July 4, 1776 The Second Continental Congress pens the Declaration of Independence.

July 31, 1776 Francis Salvador dies in battle.

August 27, 1776 The Continental army is unable to defend Long Island, and the British take New York City.

December 23, 1776 Thomas Paine publishes *The American Crisis, Number One*.

December 25–26, 1776 Washington's surprise crossing of the frozen Delaware River results in the capture of Trenton, New Jersey.

January 3, 1777 The Americans defeat the British at Princeton, forcing them to give up western New Jersey.

April 26, 1777 Sixteen-year-old Sybil Ludington alerts her father's militia that the British are burning Danbury, Connecticut.

September 11, 1777 The Americans retreat at Brandywine Crossing, Pennsylvania.

September 26, 1777 The British, under General Howe, occupy Philadelphia.

October 17, 1777 The Americans, commanded by General Horatio Gates, defeat British General John Burgoyne at Saratoga, New York.

November 15, 1777 Seven states sign the Articles of Confederation.

1777–1778 The Americans winter at Valley Forge, Pennsylvania.

June 15, 1778 The British evacuate Philadelphia.

August 20, 1778 The Supreme Executive Council of the Second Continental Congress seizes Grace Growden Galloway's home in Philadelphia.

June 21, 1779 Spain enters the war against Great Britain in an agreement with France.

May 12, 1780 The British take Charlestown (Charleston), South Carolina.

October 7, 1780 Americans retaliate against Colonel Banastre Tarleton at Kings Mountain, South Carolina.

January 30, 1781 Congress ratifies the Articles of Confederation.

March 15, 1781 The British surrender at Guilford Courthouse and give up most of North Carolina.

October 17, 1781 American troops defeat the British army at Yorktown. Cornwallis surrenders, and the war is unofficially over.

April 1782 Peace talks begin in Paris.

May 23, 1782 Robert Shurtliff enlists in the Continental army.

June 20, 1782 The Great Seal of the United States becomes official.

November 1782 Final terms for the peace treaty between the United States and England are agreed upon in Paris.

September 3, 1783 The peace treaty is signed in Paris. Britain recognizes the United States as an independent nation.

November 30, 1786 James Armistead petitions the General Assembly of Virginia for his freedom, which they award later that session. He takes the surname Lafayette in honor of the Marquis de Lafayette.

September 18, 1787 The Constitutional Convention forwards a new constitution to Congress and the states for ratification.

June 23, 1788 New Hampshire becomes the ninth state to ratify the Constitution. Now ratified by three-quarters of the states, the Constitution becomes law.

February 4, 1789 George Washington is elected the first president of the United States.

ACKNOWLEDGMENTS

The real-life accounts upon which we based this book were found in diaries, letters, and interviews, and in newspaper articles and books written by historians who spent years researching the past to create the most accurate picture. We compared sources to give the most truthful accounts of each event. During the Revolutionary era, words were spelled as they sounded and capitalized as the writer saw fit. Different writers spelled words differently. When using original source material, we changed paragraphing, punctuation, and spelling for readability. Letters have been shortened without changing their meanings. Refer to the Selected Research Sources, following this section, for more information about the books we used. We thank Dr. Christopher Collier, Connecticut state historian and professor emeritus of history at the University of Connecticut, for critiquing the manuscript; Sharon Harrison for her superb research skills and early editorial eye; and Gareth Morrow for his special reading expertise.

The Soldier with the Pen: Peter Brown

Everything in this story happened as described. Especially helpful were *Now We Are Enemies* and William Marsh's article in *Command* magazine (Jan–Feb 1995). Many thanks to Chris Perrello, editor of *Command*, for his reading and fact checking. The Battle of Bunker Hill has been well documented by eyewitnesses such as

Peter Brown and by historians. We compared various sources to create the most accurate picture. The letter quoted from Peter Brown is a shortened version of his original; you can find the original letter at the Massachusetts Historical Society's website.

The Oath: Francis Salvador

We give particular thanks to Barbara Karesh Stender, research curator, Jewish Heritage Project, Special Collections Library, the College of Charleston, for her diligent research and critiquing of the manuscript. We are also grateful to Dale Rosengarten, the library's curator of exhibitions. William Tennent's diaries, in Gibbes's *Documentary History of the American Revolution,* and William Henry Drayton's memoirs told of the efforts to get signatures in the backcountry. The events of this story are true. A meeting took place at Fort Boone on August 31, 1775, and Tennent spoke for two hours. He wrote in his diary that he quoted from the Bible but did not say which passages. His diary showed that at a similar meeting on August 13, 1775, he quoted from Mark 4:1–9, and that at a meeting on August 27, 1775, he quoted from Nehemiah 2:3. We included portions of the two passages from *The HarperCollins Study Bible* (see Meeks as editor in Selected Research Sources). It seems likely that Tennent used them repeatedly. At the August 31 meeting, Francis Salvador and Harris seconded Tennent's motion to have people sign the oath. The rest of the dialogue is based on typical arguments reported from similar meetings.

Additional thanks to Alvin Feltman of the USDA Forest Service, Long Cane Ranger District, and Jim Eden, outdoor writer and owner of the Little River Plantation, for their help with topographical details about the South Carolina backcountry.

"Yours, Portia": Abigail Adams

The events in this story were drawn from the correspondence of Abigail and John Adams and biographies by prominent historians. Anne Decker Cecere, associate editor of *The Adams Papers* at the Massachusetts Historical Society, provided much information about the Adams family and colonial life in Boston and Braintree.

Abigail and John Adams exchanged more than twelve hundred letters, detailing their daily lives and thoughts. John wrote Abigail of all the happenings in Congress. Abigail wrote about the family and business. She described many of the events in this story. She also wrote about political goings-on in Boston and of Washington's triumph in rousting the British from the city. The three letters in this story were edited from originals. We used Abigail and John's correspondence to depict a typical family evening. The dialogue was based on their letters, which showed how the family members responded to events and to one another. We relied principally on the letters found in Butterfield's *Adams Family Correspondence*. Abigail and John's letters are also housed at the Massachusetts Historical Society, American

Antiquarian Society, New-York Historical Society, and the Boston Public Library.

On August 19, 1774, Abigail Adams wrote to her husband, John, about how John Quincy (Johnny) read one or two pages each day from Charles Rollin's *Ancient History*. Johnny had been doing so since he was seven. Since his ideas about government were respected by John Adams, we surmised that Abigail also would have read *The Histories* by Polybius with her children. To learn more about Scipio, use the website provided in Books and Websites.

The Decision: George Washington

The Battle of Trenton has been well documented by people who were there and by historians. Everything in this story happened as described. George Washington and other soldiers wrote about the crossing and the battle. We compared these sources to create the most accurate picture. The dialogue was taken directly from diaries and recollections of soldiers. Among the first-hand accounts used were Alexander Graydon's *Memoirs of His Own Time*; Thomas Rodney's *The Diary of Captain Thomas Rodney, 1776–1777*; John Greenwood's *The Revolutionary Services of John Greenwood of Boston and New York*; and James Wilkinson's *Memories of My Own Times*. Thomas Paine's words were shortened from his original essay in *The American Crisis, Number One*, published December 23, 1776. We did not find mention of Thomas Paine's speech being read to the troops in any of our primary source documents, but the reference librarian at McKonkey's Ferry assured us that it is commonly held that Paine's words were read.

The crossing of the Delaware is documented in hundreds of books. *The Winter Soldiers* exquisitely details the preparation for the battle, the battle, and the aftermath. *The Day Is Ours!* is rich in primary source documents. In writing this selection, we depended on many soldiers' recollections. Special thanks to Chris Perrello, editor of *Command*, for his fact checking.

Tarnation Sybil!: Sybil Ludington

The details of Sybil Ludington's ride are documented by historians, but there is no historical record of her words or her family's words during this incident. As with all dialogue in this story, Sybil's exclamations of "Tarnation!" are fictionalized. It does seem likely, given her personality, that she would have used this "cuss" of the day. Richard Light, a distant relative of Sybil's and Nodjia's, and author Vincent Dacquino provided us with much information that was passed down through the generations to help us understand Sybil's thoughts before and during the ride and the involvement of Colonel Henry Ludington. We retraced Sybil Ludington's forty-mile route through historical accounts. The dirt roads and paths through the woods no longer exist. Today's roads allow one to cover the ride in under thirty miles, since it is necessary to travel by highway or state road for most of the ride.

Information about Sybil Ludington was also provided by Richard

Othmer of Kent, New York; historian Richard Muscarella of Putnam County, New York; Mrs. Margaret Kelso of Trenton, New Jersey; and Mrs. Carol Russell of the Wilton (Connecticut) Historical Society. They all work to keep Sybil's memory alive. The patriotic ballad "Free America," set to the tune of "British Grenadiers," was written by Joseph Warren of Boston, who died at the Battle of Bunker Hill. The ballad was published in 1909 by The Chapple Publishing Company, Ltd., Boston, in the book *Heart Songs*.

A Question of Justice: Grace Growden Galloway

Everything in this story happened as described. All of Grace Galloway's feelings, thoughts, conversations, and actions come directly from her diary. Grace Growden Galloway's diary was found in *Pennsylvania Magazine*, vol. 55, 1931–34. She wrote in great detail about her daily life from when the British left Philadelphia to just before her death. The dialogue between her and Charles Willson Peale is as she notated it in her diary. The letter to her daughter we quoted is a shortened version of the original.

The Spy: James Armistead

Historians Benjamin Quarles and Burke Davis, and deputy director Rick Schroeder and historian David Robarge, military intelligence experts at the Center for the Study of Intelligence, Washington, D.C., validated Armistead's work as a spy. We have no evidence of the actual code for the note that James delivered to the spy at Benedict Arnold's headquarters; however, we know that such notes were written in code to protect the person carrying them and the information itself in case the notes were found by the enemy. There are no historical records of exactly what information James Armistead brought to Lafayette. In trying to figure out what kinds of actions James might have taken, we spoke with experts and historians and read numerous books about life for enslaved African Americans on Virginia plantations at that time. The descriptions of the Virginia landscape, Williamsburg, the British camp, the snaring of the hog, and the stunning of the fish are accurate for the era. We created scenes based on extensive research of what a typical forager would do. The dialogue was fictionalized.

We wish to thank the many people who answered our questions about the topography and wildlife of Virginia and the likely foraging activities of a slave-turned-spy in 1781—Joe Haines, fish and game officer, Bridgeport Hydraulic Company (Connecticut); Jacquelin G. Pomeroy, New Kent County (Virginia) Historical Society; Lou Powers and Patricia Gibbs, Colonial Williamsburg Foundation; Ed Ayers, Jamestown-Yorktown Foundation; Tim Cross, planning officer for the County of York, Virginia; Diane Depew, historian, the Mariner's Museum, Newport News, Virginia; and Theresa Roane, research librarian at the Valentine Museum, Richmond, Virginia. A newspaper account in 1824 mentioned Lafayette's embrace of Armistead. Special thanks to Joe Haines,

Jacquelin Pomeroy, and Dorothy Carter, professor emeritus of children's literature, Bank Street College of Education, for their prepublication reading.

The Recruit: Robert Shurtliff

Many facts about Deborah Samson's life still remain unknown. Most of the people who wrote biographies or biographical sketches about Samson based their books on Herman Mann's book, which is riddled with inaccuracies, imagined events, and melodrama. Patrick J. Leonard led us to the most accurate book on Samson, the recently revised *Deborah Samson, Alias Robert Shurtliff, Revolutionary War Soldier*, written by Emil F. Guba. Dr. Guba addresses all the factual errors perpetuated in articles, books, and monographs about Samson. We limited our story to what we could verify in the hope that you will look at other books about Samson more critically.

SELECTED RESEARCH SOURCES

Acomb, Evelyn M., trans. *The Revolutionary Journal of Baron Ludwig von Closen 1780–1783*. Chapel Hill: University of North Carolina Press, 1958.

Briggs, Berta N. *Charles Willson Peale, Artist and Patriot*. New York: McGraw-Hill, 1952.

Butterfield, L. H., ed. *Adams Family Correspondence*. The Adams Papers, series II. Cambridge, MA: Harvard University Press, Belknap Press, 1963.

Dacquino, V. T. *Sybil Ludington: The Call to Arms*. Fleishmanns, NY: Purple Mountain Press, 2000.

Dann, John C. *The Revolution Remembered: Eyewitness Accounts of the War for Independence*. Chicago: University of Chicago Press, 1980.

Drayton, John. *Memoirs of the American Revolution as Relating to the State of South Carolina*. New York: Arno Press, 1969.

Dwyer, William M. *The Day Is Ours!: An Inside View of the Battles of Trenton and Princeton, November 1776–January 1777*. New Brunswick, NJ: Rutgers University Press, 1983.

Eckenrode, H. J. *The Revolution in Virginia*. Hamden, CT: Archon Books, 1964.

Ferling, John E. *Joseph Galloway and the American Revolution*. University Park: Pennsylvania State University Press, 1977.

Fleming, Thomas J. *Now We Are Enemies*. New York: St. Martin's Press, 1960.

Frey, Sylvia R. *Water from the Rock, Black Resistance in a Revolutionary Age*. Princeton, NJ: Princeton University Press, 1991.

Gabaldon, Diana. *Drums of Autumn*. New York: Delacorte Press, 1997.

Gelles, Edith B. *Portia: The World of Abigail Adams*. Indianapolis: Indiana University Press, 1992.

Gibbes, R. W., M.D. *Documentary History of the American Revolution*. New York: D. Appleton, 1855.

Gottschalk, Louis. *Lafayette Joins the American Army*. Chicago: University of Chicago Press, 1965.

Graydon, Alexander. *Memoir of His Own Time*. New York: Arno Press, 1969.

Graymont, Barbara. *The Iroquois in the American Revolution*. Syracuse, NY: Syracuse University Press, 1972.

Greenwood, John. *The Revolutionary Services of John Greenwood of Boston and New York*. New York: The DeVinne Press, 1922.

Guba, Emil F. *Deborah Samson, Alias Robert Shurtliff, Revolutionary War Soldier*. Plymouth, MA: Jones River Press, 2002.

Kaplan, Sidney, and Emma Nogrady Kaplan. *The Black Presence in the Era of the American Revolution*. Amherst: University of Massachusetts Press, 1989.

Karp, Abraham J., ed. *The Jewish Experience in America*. Vol. I. Waltham, MA: American Jewish Historical Society, 1969.

Kelsay, Isabel Thompson. *Joseph Brant 1743–1807: Man of Two Worlds*. Syracuse, NY: Syracuse University Press, 1984.

Ketchum, Richard M. *The Winter Soldiers*. New York: Henry Holt, 1973.

Kuntzleman, Oliver. *Joseph Galloway, Loyalist*. Philadelphia: Temple University Press, 1941.

Lefferts, Lt. Charles M. *Uniforms of the American, British, French, and German Armies in the War of the American Revolution 1775–1783*. New York: The New-York Historical Society, 1926.

Leonard, Elizabeth D. *All the Daring of a Soldier: Women of the Civil War Armies*. New York: W. W. Norton, 1999.

Leonard, Patrick J. "As Private Robert Shurtliff, Deborah Sampson [sic] served 18 months in the Continental Army." *Military History* (April 2001): 16–24.

Mann, Herman. *The Female Review: Life of Deborah Sampson* [sic]*; the Female Soldier in the War of Revolution*. New York: Arno Press, 1972.

Marcus, Jacob Rader. *Early American Jewry: The Jews of Pennsylvania and the South*. Philadelphia: The Jewish Publication Society of America, 1953.

Marrin, Albert. *The War for Independence*. New York: Atheneum, 1988.

Marsh, William. "Bunker Hill: A Dear Bought Victory." *Command* 32 (Jan/Feb 1995): 12–29.

McCullough, David. *John Adams*. New York: Simon & Schuster, 2001.

Meeks, Wayne A., ed. *The HarperCollins Study Bible. New Revised Standard Version*. New York: HarperCollins, 1989.

Meltzer, Milton. *The American Revolutionaries: A History in Their Own Words, 1750–1800*. New York: Harper, 1987.

Quarles, Benjamin. *The Negro in the American Revolution*. New York: W. W. Norton, 1973.

Rodney, Thomas. *The Diary of Captain Thomas Rodney, 1776–1777*. Reprint. New York: DaCapo Press, 1974.

Salmon, John. "A Mission of the Most Secret and Important Kind, James Lafayette and American Espionage in 1781." *Virginia Cavalcade* 31, no. 2: 78–85.

Stokesbury, James L. *A Short History of the American Revolution*. New York: William Morrow, 1991.

Tuchman, Barbara W. *The First Salute*. New York: Ballantine Books, 1988.

Waller, John H. "Slave turned double agent James Armistead Lafayette risked his life for America's freedom—and, eventually, his own." *Military History* (August 1994): 10–18.

Wilkinson, James. *Memories of My Own Times*. Philadelphia, 1816.

BOOKS AND WEBSITES
FOR YOUNG READERS

If you would like to read more about the American Revolution, you might enjoy:

Nonfiction

Bober, Natalie S. *Abigail Adams: Witness to a Revolution*. New York: Aladdin, 1995.

Carter, Alden R. *The American Revolution*. New York: Franklin Watts, 1992.

Collier, Christopher, and James Lincoln Collier. *The American Revolution: 1763–1783*. Tarrytown, NY: Marshall Cavendish, 1998.

Cox, Clinton. *Come All You Brave Soldiers: Blacks in the Revolutionary War*. New York: Scholastic, 1999.

Freedman, Russell. *Give Me Liberty: The Story of the Declaration of Independence*. New York: Holiday House, 2000.

Fritz, Jean. *Can't You Make Them Behave, King George?* New York: Putnam, 1996.

Hakim, Joy. *A History of the U.S.: From Colonies to Country 1710–1791*. New York: Oxford University Press, 1999.

Horn, Pierre L. *Marquis de Lafayette*. New York: Chelsea House, 1989.

Marrin, Albert. *George Washington and the Founding of a Nation*. New York: Dutton, 2001.

Moore, Kay. *If You Lived at the Time of the American Revolution*. New York: Scholastic, 1997.

Murphy, Jim. *A Young Patriot: The American Revolution as Experienced by One Boy*. New York: Clarion, 1996.

Peacock, Louise. *Crossing the Delaware: A History in Many Voices*. New York: Atheneum, 1998.

Fiction

Collier, James Lincoln, and Christopher Collier. *My Brother Sam Is Dead*. New York: Four Winds Press, 1974.

———. *War Comes to Willy Freeman*. New York: Delacorte, 1983.

Moss, Marissa. *Emma's Journal: The Story of a Colonial Girl*. San Diego: Silver Whistle, 1999.

Nixon, Joan Lowery. *Ann's Story: 1747*. Young Americans, Colonial Williamsburg. New York: Delacorte Press, 2000.

———. *Caesar's Story: 1759*. Young Americans, Colonial Williamsburg. New York: Delacorte Press, 2000.

Rinaldi, Ann. *Time Enough for Drums*. New York: Holiday House, 1986.

Wisler, G. Clifton. *Kings Mountain*. New York: HarperCollins, 2002.

Websites

"The Adams Papers" (Massachusetts Historical Society)
www.masshist.org/adams.html

A Biography of Thomas Paine: "The American Crisis"
odur.let.rug.nl/~usa/B/tpaine/paine.htm

Bunker Hill Exhibit (Massachusetts Historical Society)
www.masshist.org/bh/brown.html

CIA Kids Page
www.odci.gov/cia/ciakids/history

Colonial Williamsburg Foundation
www.colonialwilliamsburg.org/history/index.cfm

***Encyclopedia of American History* Time Line**
memory.loc.gov/ammem/bdsds/timeline.html

Eyewitness Account of the Battle of Trenton
www.state.nj.us/state/history/trenton.html

The Life of Hannibal Barca
www.barca.fsnet.co.uk/hannibal-barca.htm

Just for Kids
www.jvstory.com/justforkids.htm

Long Cane Ranger District (South Carolina Department of Transportation)
www.fs.fed.us/r8/fms/welcome/lc.htm

On-line Institute for Advanced Loyalist Studies
www.royalprovincial.com/military/milit.htm

Ramsay's History of South Carolina from Its First Settlement in 1670 to the Year 1808
homepages.rootsweb.com/~lynneb/Ramsayhist.html

Women of the American Revolution: The Diaries of Grace Galloway
info-center.ccit.arizona.edu/~ws/ws200/fall97/grp11/part7.htm

INDEX